To
the Mem

Michael Swinton Brown

his mother **Helen** and father **William**

---oOo---

Can we ever convey the honest depth's of our sorrows ?
The profound extent of which can match their tragic loss:
Will we dare! Open up what's in our heart and soul?
And lament such guilt and shame belongs to us.

D. J. C

Dark Skies Over School Wynd

First Published 1998 by Dominic J. Currie

Printed and bound in Great Britain
by McGilvray Printers Kirkcaldy

Front Cover Picture: The Old Lavatory in School Wynd

Copyright (C) Dominic J. Currie 1997

All rights reserved. No part of this publication may be produced, stored in a retrieval system, or transmitted in any form or by any means, electronic, mechanical, photocopying, recording or otherwise, without the prior permission of the publishers.

This book is sold subject to the condition that it shall not, by way of trade or otherwise, be lent, re-sold, hired out or otherwise circulated without the publisher's prior permission in any form of binding or cover other than that which it is published and without a similar condition including this condition being imposed on the subsequent purchaser.

ISBN 0 9532624 0 5

Acknowledgements

So many people have helped throughout the various stages in the shaping of this book that it would not be possible to thank them all individually.

However I am particularly indebted to:-

Bella Cormie of Coaltown of Wemyss who at 96 has a memory like a reference library and helped me immensely with my work. Alex Johnston of Leven, nephew of Michael Brown, who at 90 gave me every help and co-operation required. Helen L. Reading, Milford America, neice of Michael Brown; Stuart Mathewson, Leven for his encouragement and skilful photography: Eliza Bell, Cupar: Tom Carmichael, Buckhaven: Nettie Davidson, Leslie: Betty Combe, East Wemyss: Ann Watters, Kirkcaldy: Hamish Brown, Burntisland; Robert S. Roberts, St Monans: Eric Eunson, Leven; The Scottish Record Office, Edinburgh: Susan C. Payne, Principal Officer of Human History, Perth Museum: The Bell Library, Perth: Manchester Central Library: Kirkcaldy Central Library and also to the people of East Wemyss who still hold dear to their culture of faith in ordinary people.

Lastly, but by no means least, I thank my wife, Lynda, who sustained me in my work with her compliance and understanding and for my son, Owen, and daughter, Nina, who were abandoned by me for endless weekends and evenings while I was searching, sifting and writing.

Dominic J. Currie 1998

CONTENTS

Title	Page
Introduction	**1**
Black Friday	**3**
The Wemyss Murder	**10**
A Grim Discovery	**14**
Hue and Cry	**20**
The Funeral	**27**
The Sharp Eyed Peddler	**34**
A Charge of Murder	**39**
Sentence of Death	**46**
Memento-mori	**52**

Dark Skies Over School Wynd

Introduction

All murders are nasty, brutal and horrible but even then there are some crimes which are so evil and sickening that they dwarf the others even in this world of nightmares. On Saturday 20th February 1909, one national daily newspaper described the murder in East Wemyss as, "one of the most revolting that has ever occurred in Fifeshire." The local 'Wemyss Advertiser' called it "a tragedy without parallel in the history of crime in this county of Fife."

The unlikely year of 1909 began with a flurry of events which rendered it monumental for a very long time. In January an earthquake in Italy killed over 150,000 people. In London, a large number of Suffragettes attempting to win the vote for women were being unceremoniously arrested while at the same time news of yet another mining disaster was beginning to emerge. In February, at a pit in West Stanley, Durham, 163 men and boys were killed by an explosion of firedamp down the coal mine. The owners of the colliery sent food and, incredibly, champagne, in readiness for the survivors. On the day of the funerals 267 miners at Mainsforth Colliery were fined ten shillings for leaving work to attend the mass funeral of their comrades. Nearer to home a possible disaster at the Rosie pit in East Wemyss was only averted by the quick thinking of a young miner on his way to work when he noticed smoke rising from behind one of the bings. A few miles along the coast the New Wellesley Colliery had struck coal in one of its

Dark Skies Over School Wynd

two new shafts sunk at a depth of 200 fathoms. Lady Eva Wemyss, of Wemyss Castle, was preparing to lay the foundation stone for the new, much needed, Wemyss Memorial Hospital while her son Michael Wemyss of Wemyss and Torrie was preparing to celebrate his 21st birthday with a round of golf, his favourite sport. The village's of Wemyss learned of these events with solemn respect and indifference; until the day of Friday 19th February. That was the day that the heart of the small village of East Wemyss was torn out by a tragedy more real than anything they had ever read about in their newspapers or heard on their narrow street corners. This was an event which intruded into their souls and into their lives. An event so shocking that for many years it raped the moral character of a village which had been so renowned for its righteousness and integrity.

The event .... the brutal murder of the young exploited East Wemyss boy, Michael Swinton Brown; a name that even today haunts the small village of East Wemyss.

We must never be allowed to forget events and lessons from our past which scream out with the injustices of a society which cared more about its grand buildings and ceremonies than the health, safety and welfare of its workers. As with my previous publication **'The Methil Maverick'** I have tried to bring to life a period of local history which I consider to be of important educational value and one which may have otherwise been lost to posterity. Although one or two names of the trial witnesses have been changed to avoid discomfort to relatives the rest of the story is based on actual facts surrounding the Wemyss Murder.

Dominic J. Currie 1998.

Dark Skies Over School Wynd

Michael Swinton Brown (Mickey) The boy who had his very promising future snatched away from him through complacency, exploitation and finally murder.

Dark Skies Over School Wynd

Black Friday

Michael Swinton Brown, 'Mickey' as he was known locally was a small, cheerful and very popular figure in the quiet mining village of East Wemyss. He was adored by his parents William and Helen Brown who had previously lost two of their infant children to meningitis. On the 5th, April 1893 fears turned to joy as they saw Mickey develop and grow to youthful maturity. They were relieved and proud when their son left the small Wemyss village school in 1907 to pursue a career away from the busy coal mining industry and into the 'safe' working world of administration at the local linen factory. G. & J. Johnston, Linen Manufacturers on the shores of East Wemyss had been established since 1825 and had become one of the largest employers in Wemyss outside of the mining industry. By 1909 they were still a large size operation and even with the faster looms in operation the factory still had a workforce of well over 200 operators and staff. 'Mickey' Brown began working at the Johnston's factory straight from school as an office boy in July 1907. It couldn't have been better, just a few hundred yards from his home it was the ideal start he and his parents had been hoping for. Between Mickey's home and the factory where he worked lay a narrow strip of steep roadway called School Wynd which links the old village of East Wemyss on the low road with the more modern part of the village on the high road. On the left side of this walkway going down was the East Wemyss village school where young 'Mickey' did so well in his studies. On the opposite side a few yards down the road stood the forbidding and roofless public lavatory.

Dark Skies Over School Wynd

The bridge adjoining the lavatory once marked the boundary of the Wemyss estate and crossed a small burn which was known as the 'Black Burn.'

On that fateful and tragic morning of Friday 19th February, 1909, Mickey was looking forward to his sixteenth birthday which was only a few weeks away. He left his home as usual to make the short journey from his house at Parkhill Terrace, Station Road, East Wemyss to Johnston's factory on the sea shore where he worked as office boy. He looked very efficient in his dark suit, cap, tie and polished boots. Glancing at his silver pocket watch, which was a gift from his parents for his new job, he noted the time, 7.45 a.m. He turned to his mother and father and said goodbye; he shouted that he would be home at the usual time of around 12.30 p.m. for his dinner and left.

His mother half watched him whistling his way towards School Wynd from the scullery window to his work at the factory.

A short distance from Michael's house at the 'East End' of the village, Alexander Edmonstone, a twenty three year old Carter, formerly from Edinburgh but now residing in East Wemyss with his family, had risen unusually early from his bed that morning. Unusually cheerful and very excited he made breakfast for his mother and sister. Following a short conversation, he told his mother that he "may be going away for a while" if he was successful in getting a job on a steamer at Methil dock, as a boat hand, going back and forward between Methil and Hamburg. He said that if he did get a boat with the tide she was not to worry and that he would send her a postcard. After playing with his sister's child and promising to bring it a toy from

Dark Skies Over School Wynd

Hamburg he gently sang it to sleep and made ready to leave for Methil Dock. Before leaving the house he gathered up a few personal belongings and made his way to the door. Turning to his mother he said, "well mother if I mean to get a boat with the tide, it's time I was away" and off he went.

Mickey Brown had now worked two years for Johnston's linen factory and had, through his hard work, gained the position of apprentice clerk which, along with a small increase in pay, brought some added responsibilities. One such responsibility was to collect the wages from the bank at the neighbouring town of Buckhaven every Friday to pay the workers. To do this his instructions, from the senior manager James Johnston, were simple; go to the bank by tramcar, withdraw the cash and return by tramcar. Prior to the days of the tramcar, the clerk's journey was a precarious one along to the bank and back via the sea shore with the wages anything up to £300. It was a journey which had been made a hundred times before without incident; but that made it no less of a perilous journey for the solitary and merciless individual that was now expected to carry it out. No police escort, no guidelines for emergencies and no procedures in place if he didn't arrive back on time; nothing.

The long habit of not thinking the practice wrong gave it the superficial appearance of being right, and consequently raised a formidable outcry in defence of the custom in the later weeks and months.

'Folly and Innocence were so alike.
The difference, though essential, failed to strike.'

At the appointed time of 10.30 a.m. Mickey went as usual to 'Red Crag' the house of the 65 year old James

Dark Skies Over School Wynd

Johnston senior partner of the firm which was situated on the east side of the factory to collect the closed envelope containing the bank book and cheque payable to Mickey on order for the sum of £85.

A lot of money for the year 1909. Ominously, it was the very last cheque in the book. He caught the tramcar and arrived at the Royal Bank of Scotland in Randolph Street, Buckhaven at the usual time of about 11.20 a.m.

He was served by the accountant Alex Lawson, who knew Mickey and recalled him arriving at that time. He made the transaction and collected the brown leather bag which contained the following cash: £25 in one pound notes. £20 in half sovereigns. £40 in silver. The silver was made up in a long canvas bag in parcels of five pounds each separated by means of brass rings. One of the pounds were made up of sixpences. Mickey then left the bank at 11.30 a.m. to catch the 11.45 a.m. tramcar from Buckhaven to East Wemyss.

While Mickey Brown had been inside the bank transacting the business, his every move had been closely watched from across the road outside. Alex Edmonstone the twenty three year old former miner from East Wemyss had been out of work for six weeks after having recently been sacked for undisciplined behaviour from the small brewery at east brae in East Wemyss where he had worked alongside his father. Edmonstone's attitude disclosed a fundamental volatility to his mood and his mind. He was capable of deep sensitivity one moment and outrageous behaviour the next. He had left the pits for good in early February 1909 after complaining about pains in his head. These attacks had become a common complaint since July

Dark Skies Over School Wynd

1908 and were often followed by spells of dizziness and delusion. He was often heard to say that, "death would be better than these pains" and would on occasion beg someone to "knock him over the head" to end it all. His grandfather, a registered lunatic, had died as a patient in Morningside Asylum many years previous; one of the facts which was seized on later.

    Henry Kildair, a 27 year old miner from Buckhaven knew Edmonstone and had seen him standing at the corner opposite the Bank at a point where he could see anyone coming from the bank. Kildair went over and spoke to Edmonstone.

    The conversation was brief and casual and was mainly about work. At about 11.35 a.m. Edmonstone suddenly cut short the conversation and said that he was going to catch the tram home. In truth he had now spotted Mickey Brown coming from the bank with the wages and making his way to Station Road for the 11.45 tramcar to East Wemyss. James Goldie had been walking to Methil from East Wemyss that morning and had seen both Edmonstone, whom he knew, and Brown who he knew by sight at about 11.40 halfway between Muiredge pit and Station Road. According to Goldie both of them were walking along the tramlines together towards Muiredge where the trains normally stopped for passengers. The number one tramcar was on time as it pulled up at Muiredge Stopping place. Peter Adamson, a young fourteen year old colliery message boy remembered his friend 'Mickey' Brown get on the tramcar at 11.45 a.m. looking solemn and holding tightly to a brown leather bag. He also remembered Edmonstone boarding the tramcar behind Brown. Young Peter Adamson

Dark Skies Over School Wynd

continued on the tramcar as far as the Rosie pit in East Wemyss where he got off leaving Brown and Edmonstone and a young girl still in the tramcar.

Alex Chalmers the tram conductor on the number one that day from Leven remembered a boy and a man leaving the tram at Station Road at the top of School Wynd. He did not know who they were but did remember that the man had reddish brown hair. The stop at Station Road was about one minutes run from the East Wemyss car shed where the tram was due at 11.55 a.m. "They both left the tram at exactly11.54a.m. The boy being first to leave the man following close behind" said Chalmers.

As Mickey made his way down School Wynd he was just a few yards in front of Edmonstone. The final few moments of Young Mickey's life on the fateful day were witnessed by a few more of the villagers one of which, Johnston Smith, a miner at the nearby Michael pit saw Michael Brown walking down School Wynd carrying the brown leather bag. At this point it seems that Edmonstone had been trying to catch up to Brown.

Smith saw the "much taller man" not too far behind Brown and walking at a fast pace. George Black, from the Back Dykes, East Wemyss knew Edmonstone and remembered walking up School Wynd that day at about 12.00 noon. Black was walking up the footpath on the right hand side and saw Edmonstone coming down on his left. When they passed each other Black spoke to him in the Fife vernacular, "Aye Eck" to which Edmonstone replied "Aye Geordie." Black noticed nothing unusual about Edmonstone who had by this time deliberately held back so as not to be seen in the company of Brown.

Dark Skies Over School Wynd

Black also remembered passing a young boy whom he did not recognise or pay much attention to about fifty yards up from the public water closet. Black then went up to the top of School Wynd where he met Johnston Smith and four others standing on the opposite side of the road. Once Edmonstone was sure that Black was passed he made haste for Mickey whom he caught up with a few yards from the public lavatory.

Even now only a few feet away from the public lavatory yet another witness saw Edmonstone and Brown.

Alice Warrender, from School Wynd was busy at her kitchen window about 12 o' clock that day. The kitchen window faced School Wynd and looked almost directly towards the urinal. Alice remembered young Michael whom she knew coming down the Wynd from the direction of the car clutching tightly to a brown leather bag. She also saw a tall young man walking with him.

Brown being on the inside of the Wynd nearest the urinal and the tall man on the outside. They were at this time only a few feet away from the public lavatory. Alice paid no particular attention to the scene and busied herself on other matters. Had she continued to look out of her window for a few moments more she would have witnessed the first violent acts of the Wemyss Murder.

Up until now people had been going about their daily business and witnessing the movements of Edmonstone everywhere; but at the time and place Edmonstone had selected for his fatal and bloody deed it seemed that no one was around at the busiest part of the village at the busiest part of the day.

Dark Skies Over School Wynd

The Wemyss Murder

For young Mickey Brown there was to be no quick end. His torment was to last for over fifteen minutes before he eventually died of a multitude of causes. The following description of events has been pieced together from various sources connected with the murder:

Edmonstone easily caught up with Mickey Brown at around twelve o' clock just a few yards from the public lavatory. He had been seen talking to the boy moments before the attack. Edmonstone knew that he had to strike now as they approached the lavatory entrance or his chance may be lost forever. He had made up his mind long before this point that if he was to get clean away with the robbery of the factory wages then Brown who knew his face must be silenced. He wasted no time in setting about the apprentice clerk from outside the public lavatory. The brutal attack was so ferocious that almost all the bones and teeth of the young boy's face were broken or fractured in the struggle. Edmonstone at 23 was a much more taller and muscular build than that of the fifteen year old boy.

The one thing that Edmonstone had not considered was the possibility that young Mickey would be difficult to deal with. Brown's loyalty to his work was matched by his grit and determination. To save the wages at first but very quickly becoming a fight for his own survival. Silencing Mickey Brown quickly and making a clean get-away with the money had all been part of Edmonstone's plan. But the lad's plucky determination and unwillingness to yield an inch only served to make Edmonstone go berserk.

Dark Skies Over School Wynd

Kicking, punching and smashing Browns head again and again off the walls of the lavatory.

As the young boy desperately struggled for life and with his blood splattered everywhere Edmonstone, on hearing footsteps outside, quickly dragged his victim into the inner chamber of the lavatory where he again carried on his vicious attack.

Not content even at this stage with making off with the money and leaving the bloodied and battered boy lying unconscious though still alive Edmonstone strangled him with a handkerchief. He even made time to tie it into a granny knot.

As the young clerk was chocking and gargling in his final attempt at survival Edmondstone once again heard loud footsteps. Mysteriously, it was at this point that Edmonstone was interrupted in his foul deed by a man from neighbouring Dysart.

Edward Ross a bakers vanman often called at East Wemyss to deliver bread. At about 12 o' clock on that day he stopped his van on the high road at the top of School Wynd. He put his feeding bag on the horse then took several standing orders to various customers down School Wynd. As he passed the public lavatory he heard a gurgling noise and the shuffling of feet coming from inside the lavatory. Deciding to take no notice he continued to deliver the bread. On his way back up School Wynd at about 12.15 he again heard strange noises coming from the lavatory. This time curiosity got the better of Ross and he went inside thus interrupting the Wemyss Murderer. What he actually saw inside was never divulged or made clear. Even years later Ross would only say that he went

Dark Skies Over School Wynd

into the lavatory (passing a large pool of blood at the entrance) "to use it" and on hearing the strange noises coming from the water closet he claimed that he thought it was only "children from the Wemyss school fooling about." The sight Ross saw when he entered the lavatory must have shocked him into fright and silence for the rest of his life.

As the national newspapers were to report; "it is almost inconceivable that such a tragedy could have been carried out without attracting the attention of someone."

To finish the boy off and to ensure his eternal silence Edmonstone dealt the final Coup de grace by stuffing the boys cap down his throat and holding it there until all struggling ceased; but still Edmonstone was not finished. He then did something which he would later live to regret. He proceeded to plunder the boys pockets and robbed him of his silver fob-watch and chain. He then coolly made his escape from the scene of the crime. As he fled the public lavatory that afternoon he left behind him a scene of such utter havoc and horror that it would sicken people the length and breadth of the country with revulsion and disgust. There was also a gut-felt determination to catch and punish the culprit in the most severe of terms. If Edmonstone had glanced back at the mayhem he had created he would have saw the body of young Mickey Brown lying sorrowfully unrecognisable. His terminal agony mocked by the degrading lavatorial setting amid the unnatural silence of the small East Wemyss village. Ironically, at the very same time as Edmonstone was picking the dead boy's pockets, police Sergeant Robert Clydesdale from Methil had just arrived at East Wemyss. Sergeant Clydesdale was on his way to see local policeman

Dark Skies Over School Wynd

P.C. Smith and had to go down School Wynd to get there. He passed by the public lavatory at the very same time as Edmonstone was preparing to leave the scene of the crime. Clydesdale, claimed he "saw or heard nothing to attract his attention."

Dark Skies Over School Wynd

The Old East Wemyss school where Mickey Brown did so well in his studies. Circa 1900.

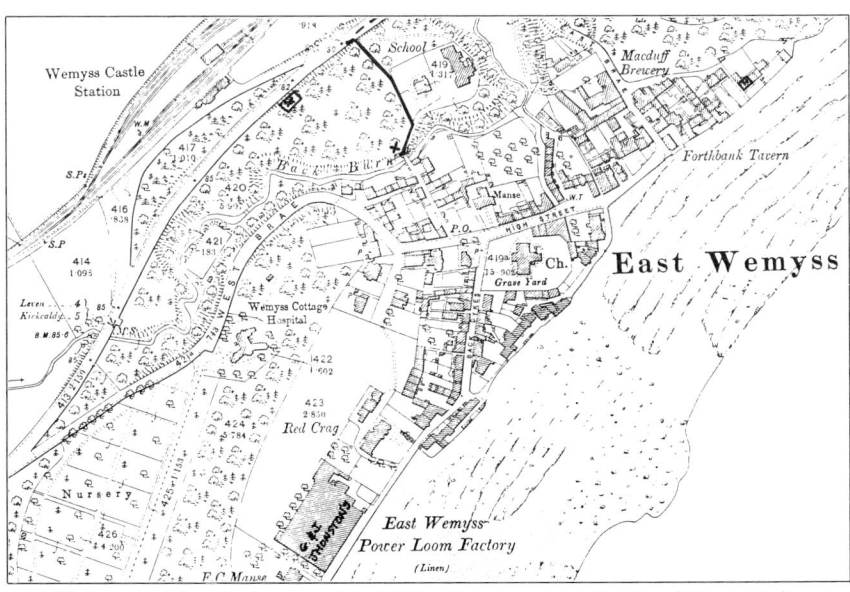

Plan of East Wemyss showing where Mickey Brown was murdered and the proximity of his house to where he worked for G.J. Johnston's.

Dark Skies Over School Wynd

Parkhill Terrace, Station Road: The home of Mickey Brown where he stayed with his mother and father, sisters and brothers.

The No 1 Tram arriving at Station Road, East Wemyss having just passed School Wynd.

Dark Skies Over School Wynd

The scene of the fateful lavatory in School Wynd taken by local photographer John Patrick just a few hours after the murder. The inner chamber and the outer door have been blocked off to the public but blood is still evident on the walls and the floor.

Dark Skies Over School Wynd

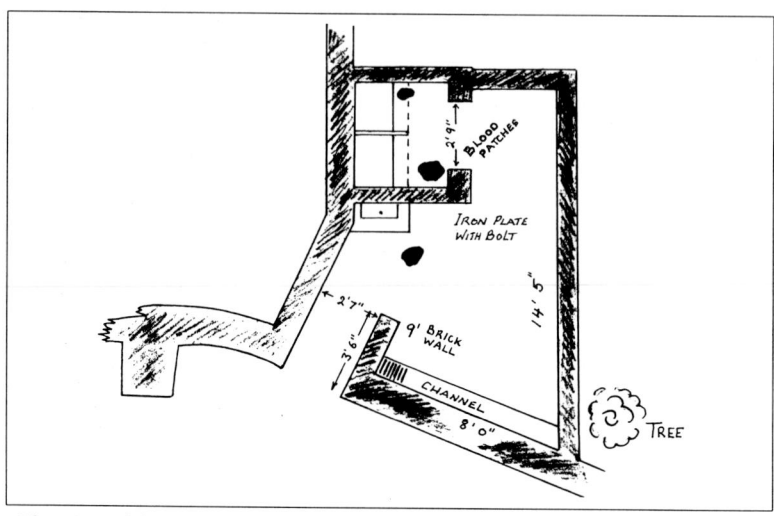

Plan view of the Lavatory showing the areas where the brutal murder took place. As seen by the plan the baker at his visit to the lavatory during the murder must have seen the blood stains on the floor as he went in; yet he denied he saw anything.

The old gates to Wemyss Cemetery. It was through here that Edmonstone made good his escape with the wages to the factory; and where Mrs Brown came to enquire as to the fate of her son.

Dark Skies Over School Wynd

A Grim Discovery

Mickey Brown usually arrived back with the wages at the factory shortly after 12 noon. Although he had still not arrived back at G & J Johnston linen works by half past twelve there was not enough concern as to his whereabouts to raise even the slightest suspicion. Even by one o' clock in the afternoon there was no alarm raised at the Factory. At five past one when J. W Johnston, senior partner of the linen works heard that a boy had been found murdered in the public lavatory, incredibly there was still no alarm raised. It was not until 1.30 p.m., one and a half hours after he was expected to arrive, that the senior partner finally realised that Mickey Brown had never returned with the wages. The other partner of the factory William R. Johnston was 'surprised' but not concerned to the point of doing anything about it until one o' clock when he was informed that a boy had been found murdered and then he 'suspected' it might be the boy Brown. William R. Johnston decided to go the local mortuary to see if it was their boy Clerk. By the time he was allowed in through the old Wemyss cemetery gate the place was buzzing with people all talking about a murder. At first William Johnston could not recognise the body. The features were so disfigured and the clothing so dirty that he failed to identify Mickey Brown because he was always so neatly dressed.

It was only after he was shown a small pencil and a tram ticket which he still held in his hand when found that he became certain that the body must be that of Michael Brown employee from the factory.

Mickey Brown's body lay motionless in the public lavatory for almost fifteen minutes before a young lad

Dark Skies Over School Wynd

named John Mulligan from nearby Approach Row who had been playing with his two friends David Morris 4 and his brother Charles 4 in School Wynd.

Mulligan walked into the lavatory and froze when he saw the battered and bloodied body of Michael Brown. He immediately ran out of the lavatory and screamed to the first man he saw to come and see. Alex Sigley from Murrie Place Leven had been about forty yards up the Wynd passed the lavatory when the young boy had shouted on him. Sigley rushed back, went inside he was horrified at the scene. He saw the lifeless body lying on its back on the floor with its head flopped against the wall nearest to School Wynd. As Sigley staggered out of the lavatory the memory of the awful sight still reeling in his mind he was easily pushed aside by the in-rushing police constable Alex Stewart who had also just been informed about the body. Stewart swiftly removed the cap from the boys mouth, undid the handkerchief from around the neck and slackened the collar and tie. Refusing to accept that the boy was beyond help Stewart hurriedly brought the boys body to the outer chamber and carefully laid him down. Although there were no signs of life Stewart still felt a natural impulse to strive for it. Tenderly cleaning blood from the boys face with his shaking hands he appealed to the growing crowds of spectators to run and fetch the local doctor. Stewart was now on his knees doing his frantic best to give the young boy artificial respiration. Moments later amid heart rendering scenes of frantic and fruitless efforts to revive young Mickey Brown a firm hand was laid on the shoulder of the distraught young constable who was by this time showing signs of emotional distress at his own failure

Dark Skies Over School Wynd

to revive the boy. Doctor Watson from Wemyss gently helped the constable to his feet and led him out. The Doctor returned to pronounce the boy dead. They estimated that about thirty or forty minutes had gone since the time of death. It was impossible for the police officers and the villagers who had now crowded around the lavatory to identify who it was lying in such a demoralised state.

Assuming that the lad was from outside the village it was decided to convey the body to the local mortuary to await identification and a post-mortem examination which the authorities were compelled to make under such circumstances. As they carried the young boy's body through the old cemetery gate towards the mortuary the gate was already lying half open having been pushed aside by the fleeing Edmonstone as part of his escape less than an hour before. Until now no one had been able to identify the body until it was shown to William Russell Johnston employer of the deceased who after much deliberation identified it as that of Michael Swinton Brown. There was now another piece of important news for the police to think about. The boy had been carrying the factory wages...and they were missing. The police now felt sure that money had been the motive for the murder and were quick to grasp the situation.

No trace could be found of the brown leather bag which had held the wages the boy had been guarding with his life.

In a small village like that of East Wemyss in 1909 news travelled very fast and within a few minutes after the discovery of the body School Wynd was a heaving mass of people. The murder held a morbid fascination of its own. Dull streets became fraught with mystery. Common

Dark Skies Over School Wynd

At the appointed time of 10.30 a.m., Mickey Brown went as usual to 'Red Craig' (above), the house of 65 year old James Johnstone, senior partner of the linen factory on the shores of East Wemyss, to collect the envelope containing the bank book and cheque payable to Mickey for the sum of £85.

On board the 11.45 a.m. tramcar as Michael Brown brought the wages from the Buckhaven bank, were his murderer Alexander Edmonstone and a 14 year old colliery message boy by the name of Peter Adamson - who later became an important witness for the prosecution.
Above: The No. 1 tram stopping at the Rosie pit in East Wemyss. It's next stop was School Wynd.

17

Dark Skies Over School Wynd

dwellings suddenly assumed a sinister expression and everyone concerned howsoever plain and ordinary was invested with a new importance as the bright red sunshine fell from the tragic seaside village.

As news reached the workers at the factory where the boy had been employed that a body had been discovered in the public lavatory and that the young clerk was 70 minutes late it became painfully apparent that the victim was that of their dear friend and comrade, wee "Mickey Broon."

Young and old downed their tools switched off their machines and made their way to the fatal spot to ask numerous probing questions. By the time the two o' clock whistle had punctually sounded for the return of the workers to the factory there was not a single step taken in the direction of the Johnston linen works by the workers that afternoon. 'Wee Mickey' their comrade and friend had just been brutally murdered. They were in no mood to resume normal working practice. Shock and sadness was mixed with anger as they discussed the circumstances of the whole affair. Having anticipated the situation and not wishing to exacerbate an already delicate situation the management decided to announce a "suspension of operations for the remainder of the day"...not a soul was there to hear it being announced. School Wynd was packed with people from all over the village and beyond. A new name was being discussed in whispers throughout the crowd. Alexander Edmonstone, from East Wemyss, last man to be seen with 'Mickey Broon' was now missing.

Meanwhile, back at Parkhill Terrace Mickey Brown's mother, Helen, was becoming quite concerned at the late arrival of her son. He would always arrive home for his

Dark Skies Over School Wynd

dinner at about 12.30 p.m. as he had done since starting at the factory. Standing concerned and looking for him from the doorway of their home less than 100 yards from the public lavatory she called to a young schoolboy who was passing and asked what all the commotion was down School Wynd. The boy mistakenly replied that a 'Buckhaven' lad had been killed.

By around 1.30 p.m. she became frantically concerned. Having heard that the body of a boy had been taken to the local mortuary at East Wemyss she set out to dispel her worse fears by going there. On reaching the cemetery gate at East Brae she found it locked and so began to make her way back home.

As she reached the top of East Brae from the cemetery gate she asked one of the many school boys running about excitedly the name of the boy who had been killed in the public lavatory.

The boys words was the realisation of all her worst nightmares. Michael's name kept ringing over and over in her head. The scene which followed was too tender for words. Mrs Brown frantic and distraught by the news collapsed and was immediately helped home by neighbours where she lay in bed completely prostrate for several days. The young boys father William Brown who had been working as a stonemason in the Coaltown of Wemyss a mile along the road was informed of the tragedy. He ran all the way home with a thousand thoughts fleeting through his mind to be with his grief stricken wife, hoping beyond hope that there had been some kind of a mistake.

Dark Skies Over School Wynd

The Bank on the corner at Buckhaven from where Mickey Brown left with the wages; he never arrived at the Johnston's Linen factory nor was there any alarm raised by the management for well over an hour and no search party sent out to find him.

Johnston's Factory where Mickey set off at 10.40 a.m. with the last cheque in the book for the wages for the workers. He never returned.

Dark Skies Over School Wynd

Alexander Edmonstone (from the Wanted Poster): A gambler by nature played for high stakes when he left his home in the East End of East Wemyss on February 19th 1909. His plea of insanity was never likely to succeed.

Dark Skies Over School Wynd

The Old Court Cave on the shores of East Wemyss where Edmonstone emptied the wages bag and planted the money around his body. Circa 1900.

MacDuff Castle where Edmonstone hid the brown leather bag which had carried the wages and the cheque book. Circa 1900.

Dark Skies Over School Wynd

The Old Mortuary hidden behind the bushes and trees on the right was where Dr Alexander Watson performed the Post Mortem on the murdered boy.

The fingerprints of young Mickey Brown taken in the mortuary at Wemyss Cemetery the day after the murder. The lavatory seat was unhinged and the prints upon that used as evidence. (S.R.O.)

Dark Skies Over School Wynd

Hue and Cry

During routine questioning it quickly came to light that a local man by the name of Edmonstone had been the last person seen with Mickey Brown prior to his murder. At once he became the prime suspect resulting in a mobilisation of minds throughout the entire police force. Every available man was called in and every other task subordinated to the hunt to find the killer. Police Sergeant Robert Clydesdale from Methil immediately went to the home of Alexander Edmonstone. A frail and shocked Mrs Edmonstone informed him that her son had not returned since leaving for Methil Dock's that morning. Following a lengthy interview and a full description of the suspect Sergeant Clydesdale asked if she had any photographs of him? She replied "yes" and went into a small carved wooden box on top of a chest of drawers in her son's bedroom. After turning over some photographs in the box she replied "that's strange, I can't find any of his photographs here." Sergeant Clydesdale asked her if she was sure that he kept his photographs in that box among the other photographs? "Yes" she replied, and added innocently that "he must have taken all of his own photographs out of the box before he left the house in the morning." Sergeant Clydesdale now felt sure he knew who the murderer was. He still required a photograph for the 'wanted poster' which he got from Edmonstone's sister. The hunt was now on for the most wanted criminal in the country.

After the murder Edmonstone avoided the main roads to make good his escape by slipping along the black burn past the school through the glen and out at the village brewery on

Dark Skies Over School Wynd

FIFESHIRE CONSTABULARY.

MURDER AND ROBBERY.

Photograph and Description of man wanted on Sheriff's Warrant charged with having, about 12.15 p.m. on Friday, 19th February curt., murdered Michael S. Brown, clerk, 16 years of age, in a public lavatory in East Wemyss, Fifeshire, and robbed him of a bag, containing—
25 One Pound Notes of the Royal Bank of Scotland, Nos. unknown ;
40 Half-Sovereigns ;
£40 in Silver, made up in canvas bags of £5 each with small brass rings round the necks.
The watch and chain the boy was wearing is also missing—
White metal keyless, white dial, black hands and numerals ; white metal chain.

ALEXANDER EDMONSTONE,

23 years of age, miner or carter, has not been at work for 6 weeks, having been dismissed from the Brewery in East Wemyss, where he had wrought, 5 feet 9 inches in height, slender built, looks and may be somewhat taller, auburn or reddish-brown hair, dark eyes, full ruddy face, clean shaved, **wants three teeth in front of upper jaw,** A. E. tattoed on right forearm, Scotch accent, native of Edinburgh, is said to have suffered last summer from mental aberration.

Dressed when he absconded in brown jacket suit, seat of trousers patched, green cap, white sweater with folding down collar, usually turned up and fastened with safety pin, black lacing boots. The clothing and boots would probably have been bloodstained.

About 5 p.m. same day accused bought the undernoted clothing at Strathmiglo, some 15 miles distant from the scene, and took train to Perth :—
Mottled yellow brown tweed Jacket Suit, cost 18s.   Dark grey "Showerproof" Coat, single-breasted, turned-over cuffs, black bone buttons, sleeve lining black, blue and white stripes, quilted round scyes, usual pockets, side pockets slanting, cost 26s 9d.   Dark grey, single-peaked (8 pieced) Cap, size 7 or 7⅛, "The Dunkeld" stamped inside black on yellow lining, cost 1s.   Dark green Silk Muffler, of white broken pattern, cost 4s 11d.   Received as a present a mauve, grey, and brown striped long Tie.

Jacket, vest, and trousers, with bloodstains at foot of both legs, have just been recovered in a boarding-house at 113 Renfrew Street, Glasgow, and identified as that worn by accused.   There was also found there a pair of braces, pair of grey socks, Kirkcaldy striped cotton shirt, white cellular shirt, and a small ornament about the size of a half-penny with shamrock upon it.   He called at this house about 11 a.m. on Saturday, 20th curt., and left 20 minutes afterwards saying he was going to meet a friend, and did not return.   Will have probably purchased fresh underclothing.

He may also continue to shave or he may not, or may otherwise alter his personal appearance, and may dye his hair.

It should also be remembered that, having regard to the publicity given to his person and clothing, he may again purchase a fresh outfit.

Will in all probability endeavour to go abroad.

It is earnestly requested that strenuous inquiry be continued at Railway Stations, Shipping Offices, Temperance Hotels, Lodging-Houses, Banks, and other likely places.   If any clue is obtained please follow up and communicate at once with me.

J. TENNANT GORDON,
Chief Constable of Fife.

Chief Constable's Office,
County Buildings, Cupar, 22nd Feb., 1909.

Wanted Poster I:
This was the first wanted poster distributed around the county at a time when the local police felt that Edmonstone's capture would only be a matter of time. (S.R.O.)

Dark Skies Over School Wynd

Strathmiglo High Street. The small drapers shop in the high street was where Edmonstone made his first purchase with the stolen money.

Perth as it looked when Edmonstone arrived off the train from Strathmiglo.

Dark Skies Over School Wynd

Mrs Helen Brown, mother of Michael sits for a photograph shortly after the murder. Mrs Brown was too distressed to attend young Michael's funeral and wore black for the rest of her life.

Dark Skies Over School Wynd

East Brae where his father was working inside oblivious of his son's actions.

Crossing the road at East Brae he made his way into Wemyss cemetery through the old gate as far as the top of the ancient Pictish Court Cave where he jumped the wall and made for the cave.

It was inside the old Court Cave that Edmonstone first examined the contents of his plunder. In ancient times it was said that the court of the cave was summoned by the ringing of a bell which hung from a hole in the roof. MacDuff, Thane of Fife is also said to have made his escape from Kennoway Castle through this cave from the clutches of Macbeth. Now, in the quietness between the cemetery and the sea Edmonstone was emptying the leather bag of its contents and distributing the money around his body so as not to attract attention. He then made his way along to the whins between the Court Cave and MacDuff Castle where he hid the leather bag in some rocks. Doubling back across the main road he then headed west.

At about 12.45 p.m. Eliza Nicholson of Newton Farm was hanging out her washing when she spotted Edmonstone coming out of the wood. His boots were very dirty and he was wiping perspiration from his face. He began to walk as though there was no cause for alarm. Edmonstone reached the parish of Falkland shortly after 3p.m. Mrs Rachel Fleming was pulling hay from a stack on her farm when she noticed Edmonstone coming along the highway from the direction of the New Inn. He asked her for a loan of a brush which she kindly obliged. While he was brushing his trousers she noticed two very darkly stained marks on both knees which he had difficulty in

Dark Skies Over School Wynd

getting out. Edmonstone said to her "I doubt if the stains will come out." He then asked her if he could get a train at Strathmiglo to Perth as he was going to see a sister there. She said that he could and after about five minutes brushing himself he left quite cool like and in no hurry.

Edmonstone was then seen approaching Strathmiglo high street by the owner of the drapers shop George Knox who was out for a stroll. Knox took little notice of the man except that he looked dishevelled and had walked a great distance. When Knox returned to his draper shop he found the same man being served by his wife inside the shop. Edmonstone turned pale as the smartly dressed Knox walked in but he soon regained his composure when he realised he was not a policeman. Shop Assistant Jane Wilkie sold him a suit of clothes costing eighteen shillings: a muffler four shillings and elevenpence and an overcoat at twenty six and ninepence. He also bought a cap which he put on his head straight away. Edmonstone said to Jane that he was going home to see his mother after running away from home ten years ago. He said that his father had since died and that he had only written five times home since he left. He said that he had been living with his aunt Mrs Lumsden in Falkland who had given him some money to go and see his mother in Perth. He paid for the clothes with three half sovereigns three crown pieces and two half crowns. She then rolled the purchased clothes into brown paper and with permission gave Edmonstone a tie as a gift for such a good sale. He put on the new overcoat and said goodbye as he left the shop. Meanwhile, in the Strathmiglo police station just a few yards away a message giving information on the Wemyss murder along with a full

Dark Skies Over School Wynd

description of the murderer lay unread on the desk awaiting the return of the duty officer from outwith the town.

Back at the Wemyss village the police were boarding up the entrance to the scene of the tragedy and organising groups of enthusiastic local volunteers to help find the murderer. Their numbers were greatly increased by the arrival of local miners from the backshift angry and eager to help in any way possible.

At about 4.20 in the afternoon one of those miners, Thomas Moodie from Wemyss, found the brown leather bag which had been stuck into a whin bush and the envelope containing the new cheque book lying open nearby just down from MacDuff Castle. Inspector Cameron motored to Methil Dock and made extensive enquiries as well as a search of all ships in dock but no trace of the suspect was found. Chief Constable Tennant Gordon and a large staff of police officers and volunteers still patrolled the Wemyss village but as the light began to fade so also did the hopes of catching the murderer.

Edmonstone's hopes were high as he made his way from the drapers shop to the booking office at Strathmiglo railway station at about 6.05 p.m. and with his muffler pulled up to his mouth he bought a ticket to Perth: the only ticket sold for Perth that afternoon. He arrived at Perth Station at about half past eight o' clock and instead of booking into a nearby hotel he walked a half mile down to Leonard Street to the modest little Temperance Hotel. He was met by the house waitress Margaret Flynn who showed him to his upstairs room number '13' which looked out onto the gas-lit front street. Edmonstone asked to be called at 7.00 a.m. and handed her his boots to be cleaned.

Dark Skies Over School Wynd

She noticed he had a lisp from the absence of three front teeth.

The boots became a talking point for the poor kitchen maid who had the job of cleaning them. She remarked to her friend about the disgraceful state they were in. Edmonstone then retired for the night to his darkened but comfortable room taking one last look out of the window before going to bed. Next morning on 20th February Margaret Flynn called to Edmonstone at 7.00 a.m. but he was already up and dressed. Following a hearty breakfast of ham and eggs Edmonstone paid his bill and was once again on the train this time heading for the busy city of Glasgow via Doune and Stirling.

A couple of hours later at 10 o' clock Perth police on making enquiries at the North British Railway booking office were told that a man answering the description of Edmonstone had booked a ticket for...'Edinburgh', which sparked off a full scale search of the Capital.

While Edmonstone was journeying to Glasgow and making plans on how best to spend his money Doctor Alexander Watson and Doctor Allan Curror were inside the grim little mortuary of East Wemyss preparing to get underway with the task of conducting the Post-mortem on the murdered body of Mickey Brown. The first sight and examination of the body revealed a sickening catalogue of injuries. They had never seen anything like it. After a few hours in the mortuary they found the cause of death to be "due to Haemorrhage and shock. Probably aggravated by attempts at strangulation." Thus Edmonstone's botched attempts at strangulating his victim had not, after all, been the cause of death. It was the severe smashing and beating

Dark Skies Over School Wynd

which had eventually taken its toll on the young boy. The reverent silence of the mortuary was broken by the gradual sounds of barking bloodhounds belonging to a Major Richardson who had on request by the Fifeshire police travelled up from London to help in the search for the fugitive. Though by this time the scent like the suspect himself had all but vanished.

By the time Edmonstone arrived at Charring Cross Station he had read the detailed reports of his deadly mission in most of the national newspapers and was, for the first time since that violent afternoon, quite perplexed and agitated. After wandering around Glasgow for a short while he called into the lodgings of Margaret Bryce 113 Renfield Street at 11.15 a.m. and asked her for a room for a couple of nights. She told him that the price would be one shilling and sixpence per night. He gave her three shillings and a sixpence.

His agitation became a panic measure to throw the police off his trail by doing two things; faking suicide; and leaving for England.

Placing his two parcels on the bed he left his lodgings saying to the landlady that he was going for a short walk to meet his pal. He never returned. Making his way to Paisley he walked to the river Cart where he carefully left a suicide note on the parapet of the bridge which crosses the river. The note, which was written in red ink, read as follows:-

"I murdered Mickey Brown - A.E.
You will find my body at the foot of water near by.
I filled my pockets with stones. I bid goodbye to mother.
Goodbye - Alexander Edmonstone

Dark Skies Over School Wynd

The police could not afford to treat the note lightly and agonised for days over the way to handle it. Back at 113 Renfield Street Mrs Bryce was more than a little curious about her new lodger. She had read the reports about the Wemyss murder in the newspapers and when Edmonstone failed to return she decided to investigate his room. Seeing the two parcels lying on the bed she undid the smaller one and found two shirts and a pair of socks. Late in the afternoon she undid the other parcel and found a suit of clothes stained with blood and informed the police immediately. By now Edmonstone was on his way by train to Manchester and was hoping that he had at last shaken off his pursuers.

Dark Skies Over School Wynd

The once 'Temperance Hotel' in Leonard Street Perth; now a social club. Edmonstone spent his first night on the run in this modest hotel. His room number 13 was ominous.

Renfield Street, Glasgow where Edmonstone began to panic and decided to fake a suicide note. Circa 1910.

Dark Skies Over School Wynd

The Funeral

At half past three on the afternoon of Monday 22nd February 1909 the funeral of Michael Brown took place. Most business' all over Wemyss was suspended and the small Public School where Mickey had attended flew its flag at half mast. Meanwhile, the schoolmaster Mr James Cassells prepared to represent the School at the funeral and say farewell to one of their brightest. J & G Johnston, the factory where Mickey had been employed, opened for work as usual until 2 p.m. The main roads were thick with pedestrians as people poured into East Wemyss from all over the country keen to pay their last respects to the boy. The road between Michael's parents house in Parkhill Terrace and the cemetery 800 yards away was packed with mourners dressed in black. There was not a house in the Wemyss that did not have a representative at the funeral. Blinds were drawn on all windows and shops shut for the day. Every moment seemed to see more and more people arrive to add to the whispering masses already there. By three o' clock the whole of the highway was lined from end to end while in the cemetery a huge square was formed by the crowd near the section of the family burial ground. Behind the crowd, just a few yards away towards the boundary wall, footprints of the murderer were still on the soil from where he had made his escape.

In broken tones a brief service was conducted in the house of the Brown family by Rev Low and Rev Kennedy. The body of young Mickey encased in a white coffin with brass mountings was a heart breaking sight to the people who watched the black hearse move slowly along the road.

Dark Skies Over School Wynd

As the cortege passed them by every head was bowed low and many subdued expressions of sympathy were heard as people gave way to their emotions. The grief stricken family minus Mrs Brown who was to distressed to attend trailed behind the coffin mourning their lost one. The coffin bore the following inscription:-

"Nothing in thy hand I bring
Simply to thy cross I cling."
Michael Brown aged fifteen years

Reverently the public fell in behind the crowds already inside the cemetery. Around the grave the relatives and friends were surrounded by between four and five thousand people most of whom barely heard the service or saw the proceedings but were nevertheless contented to be at the service and final resting place of the tragic young boy. The Rev Kennedy read the lesson and the Rev Low led in a moving prayer. Intense silence rested over all the cemetery and only the faint sounds of the restless sea could be heard against the solidity of the minister's voice. The scene of the minister stooping to comfort the distress of an anguished friend of Mickey Brown was one which would live in the memories of all those in attendance that day.

Pall-bearers were :-
Mr William Brown (Father): His two sons William and Tom: John Johnston: Thomas Brown: Charles Simpson: Michael and Charles Swinton.

Dark Skies Over School Wynd

I stood beside the little tomb,
In the graveyard near the town
Where sleeps neath wreaths of blossoms gay:
Dear little Mickey Brown.

The plaintive winds wailed 'mid the trees,
That skirt the grassy way;
While on the roof tops all around
The golden sunshine lay.

No more along the narrow street,
Or down the School Wynd lane;
Glad-hearted Mick in boyish glee,
Will ever rove again.

No more we'll press his tender hand,
Nor hear his laughter gay;
No more we'll see his smiling face,
To enrich our lives each day.

Cut off when life was bright and fair,
The work of wicked hands;
Gone from this world of struggle,
In heaven now he stands.

W. Linton 1909

Edmonstone had now vanished without trace and although a wanted poster had been issued on Monday 22nd February to most police stations throughout the country it had brought no results. By the following week the population of Fife was beginning to get very frustrated as to

Dark Skies Over School Wynd

Edmonstone's whereabouts. A letter from Henry Brown Procurator Fiscal to the Crown Agent in Cupar, demonstrates these feelings.

27th Feb. 1909
"Sir,
I am becoming anxious about this case. Local feeling is very keen and it is most important that the suspect should not escape. We have done everything that can be suggested but as yet in vain."

It goes on to say:

"The boys parents are poor folks and I doubt if his employers will undertake an indefinite liability.

I shall also be obliged if you will consider the propriety of offering a reward for information as to Edmonstone's whereabouts. He has plenty of money with him and may be lurking in some den where the people are keeping him for payment.

The offer of a reward may tempt them to give information which they may otherwise withhold.

The police will issue a new Wanted poster with a later photograph of Edmonstone which can also include the offer of the Reward if you approve.

Your Obedient Servant,
Henry W. Brown (P.F.)

On 8th March 1909 evidence of how serious they had taken the suicide note was shown when Henry Brown stated in further correspondence to the Procurator Fiscal in Cupar:

Dark Skies Over School Wynd

Sir

" There are good grounds for supposing that the recent suicide letter found at the River Cart is the genuine production of Edmonstone although of course it is probable that it was intended to mislead. If the letter is genuine it is most important that the question should be settled decidedly whether Edmonstone's body is in the River Cart or not. Every day will render it more difficult to identify the body if found.

I would respectfully suggest that if the Crown Council thinks there is a possibility of the letter being genuine they should give me instructions to have the river thoroughly searched. I would then ask the assistance of the P.F. of Renfrewshire to see the work done effectively.

Your Obedient Servant
Henry W. Brown (P.F.)

On March 25th 1909 Harry Brown reported to Cupar:

"As instructed by the Crown Council I have had the River Cart carefully dragged but no trace was found either of Edmonstone's body or the stolen property."

Having failed to detect even the slightest clue as to Edmonstone's possible location the Procurator Fiscal's mind turned to the possibility of him having left for America.

On April 7th 1909 The Chief Constable of Fifeshire wrote to the Crown Agents:

*"Dear Sir,
I send you herewith a letter of 9th from the Detective Publishing Company Chicago together with copy of their*

Dark Skies Over School Wynd

publication ' The Detective' from which it would seem they will insert a photograph and description of Edmonstone for $15 and it may be advisable to take advantage of this.

I have already sent out Wanted Posters offering £100 Reward to 'Pinkertons Detective Agency' and thirteen of the principle places in the United States; nine chief towns in the provinces of Canada and Newfoundland as well as to Australia, New Zealand and South Africa. Also on the chief ports on the Continent but notwithstanding the 'Detective' publication seems to afford an additional method of reaching directly those who are likely to take a vital interest in the matter.

Yours Sincerely
J. Tennant Gordon
(Chief Constable of Fife)

Following the funeral of Michael Brown there was deep and genuine anger that the murderer of the young boy whom the Wemyss had now buried was still at large. A second Wanted Poster was issued on 5th March 1909 and contained two photographs of the suspect Alex Edmonstone East Wemyss. The first photograph was taken in 1905 and the other was taken in November 1908. This time a bold headline of **£100 Reward** was blazoned across the top along with a full description of the suspect. This had an immediate impact; though not always the desired effect.

Following the issuing of the £100 Reward poster the police were suddenly inundated with claims of having sighted the murderer all over the country. One man in Leith Edinburgh had to run the gauntlet of an angry crowd after

Dark Skies Over School Wynd

having been arrested for the seventh time as a result of his likeness to Edmonstone. The man eventually had to go into hiding as a result of the panic and enthusiasm to catch the killer.

Newspapers were giving daily reports about the latest hunt for the killer and his frustrating ability to outwit the police since the day of the murder.

"...Perhaps he has been more lucky than clever. It is often said that the evil one is good to his own children. Certainly he has thrown his protecting cloak over the "Satan" of East Wemyss."

...Edmonstone must be got and the authorities all over the country do not hesitate to say that he shall be got. The good book say's, "Vengeance is mine; I will repay"

Reported in the local press in March 24th 1909.

From the moment that Edmonstone had fled the scene of the murder at 12.20p.m. on Friday 19th February the stolen silver watch had been steadily ticking away, and was now about to play its own part in the eventual capture of Edmonstone.

Dark Skies Over School Wynd

One of hundreds of cards produced and sold by the 'Fifeshire Advertiser' to help the Brown family meet the cost of the funeral for their son.

Dark Skies Over School Wynd

The funeral of Michael Brown taken moments after he was laid to rest on February 22nd, 1909. All classes of society were there in large numbers. Michael's father cried al throughout the service. The ruins of MacDuff Castle can be seen in the distance.

Monument from his fellow workers who walked out of the factory at the sea shore as a mark of respect for their murdered colleague, Mickey Brown.

Dark Skies Over School Wynd

£100 REWARD

MURDER AND ROBBERY.

(1)

(2)

Alex Edmonstone
(3)

WANTED, on Sheriff's Warrant, charged with having about noon on **Friday, 19th February, 1909,** murdered Michael Swinton Brown, Clerk, 16 years of age, in a Public Lavatory in **East Wemyss, County of Fife, Scotland,** and Robbed him of a Bag containing—

25 One Pound Notes of the Royal Bank of Scotland, Nos. unknown,
40 Half-Sovereigns,
£40 in Silver, made up in canvas bags of £5 each, with small brass rings round the neck;
Also White Metal Keyless Watch, white dial, black hands and numerals; white metal chain

Alexander Edmonstone,

23 years of age, Miner or Carter, 5 feet 9 inches or thereby in height, slender build, **auburn or reddish-brown hair,** dark eyes, full ruddy face, hitherto clean shaved, **wanted three teeth in front of upper jaw, A. E. tattooed on right forearm,** Scotch accent, native of Edinburgh.

(1) Photograph taken in 1906.
(2) Photograph taken in November, 1908, in carter's attire (holding horse).
(3) Signature.

Both Photographs are said by his companions to be like him. No. 1 shows the head well up, and the nose consequently appears shorter than in No. 2.

Edmonstone purchased the following new clothing: Mottled yellow brown tweed Jacket Suit; dark grey "Showerproof" Coat, single-breasted, turned-over cuffs, black bone buttons, sleeve lining black blue and white stripes, quilted round scyes, usual pockets, side pockets slanting; dark grey, single-peaked (8-pieced) Cap, size 7 or 7½, "The Dunkeld" stamped inside black on yellow lining; dark green silk Muffler, white broken pattern; mauve grey and brown striped long Tie. May be wearing this or part of it, or may have bought a fresh outfit and new boots, his old ones being well worn and shabby. A cast suit of clothing and underclothing belonging to him has been recovered in a boarding house in Glasgow.

May continue to shave or may not, may acquire artificial teeth, may dye his hair, or may otherwise change his personal appearance. Will probably endeavour to leave the country.

The above Reward will be paid by the Subscriber to any person furnishing such information as shall lead to the apprehension and conviction of the person or persons who committed said crime.

J. TENNANT GORDON,
Chief Constable of Fife.

Chief Constable's Office,
Cupar-Fife, Scotland, 5th March, 1909.

Wanted Poster II with Reward & second photograph of A. Edmonstone: This second poster was put together as a result of the frustration everyone felt at the suspects liberty and the horrific nature of the crime. (S.R.O.)

Dark Skies Over School Wynd

The Sharp Eyed Peddler

At a time when people all over the country were beginning to think that Edmonstone had got clean away he was suddenly arrested in Manchester. The result of a curious Peddler from Altwich. Following his fake suicide attempt at the River Cart in Glasgow he disappeared without trace. It was on the 1st March that Alex Edmonstone giving the name of Albert Edward's to disguise the letters 'A E' tattooed on his left arm called at a house in 12 Brunswick Street, a southern suburb of Manchester, and asking for comfortable lodgings. He had been staying at a Temperance Hotel in London Road but left because it was 'too expensive.' He had been engaged to work at a motor show at Bellevue Gardens about a mile away. His luggage consisted of a gladstone bag which during his stay at the house he always kept hidden and locked. When he was asked about it by the landlady Mrs Mary Jane Bridgewood he had replied that he "had been robbed once and had to be very careful." Shortly after his arrival at the house in Brunswick Street Manchester, Edmonstone purchased a ten shillings motor car licence again under the pseudonym of Albert Edwards. He lived a false life while staying in Manchester claiming he was working for a firm by the name of Verity.

He would go out about 9 o' clock in the morning and would turn up for his dinner about 2 o' clock. Going out again about 2.30 p.m. he would return for tea about 5 p.m. and spent his evenings visiting places of amusement and buying everyone drinks. However, people were noticing the amount of leisure time he had and were beginning to ask

Dark Skies Over School Wynd

questions. One of his ready made friends was to remark that, "judging by the way that 'Edward's' got rid of half-crowns when he could have paid in smaller change made us think he was a show-off."

But Edmonstone's luck ran out on the week of Monday 19th March when the Peddler named John Atherton arrived at the house in 12 Brunswick Street looking for lodgings. Edmonstone was not eating or sleeping very well as if he had something on his mind. Mrs Bridgewood asked Edmonstone what part of Scotland he had come from and he replied Edinburgh. She then quite innocently asked him about the murder that had taken place in Fife. "Isn't it funny that they haven't found the man who murdered that young boy yet ?" Edmonstone replied, " Yes I know; It's a sad and cruel job that !" then without saying any more went on with attempting to eat his dinner.

Atherton went to Whitworth Police station on Tuesday 20th March to make simple enquiries about a peddlers licence. As he went into the police station he noticed a Reward and Wanted poster offering £100 for the arrest of a man on suspicion of murdering a youth in Scotland. Atherton never paid much attention to it and went home after his business at the police station. On Tuesday 21st March Atherton went to complete his paperwork for his licence at the Whitworth Police station and again noticed the Wanted poster, only this time pondering on the likeness of the person in the photograph more closely and reading the full details. He fancied the face looked vaguely familiar.

On the morning of 22nd of March Atherton had a drink in the house with Edwards while all the time assimilating

Dark Skies Over School Wynd

his features. Finally, Atherton casually asked Edmonstone if he had the correct time on him. Edmonstone said yes and produced the stolen silver watch. Atherton's blood went cold. He now knew that he was looking at the man wanted for the murder of the young Scottish boy.

He then made haste to collect his peddlers licence from the police station. On this third visit to the police station by Atherton he informed the police of his very strong suspicions about the man living at his lodgings at 12 Brunswick Street. They took down every detail and said they would call round later. Atherton also told his landlady Mrs Bridgewood of his suspicions. She immediately sent her daughter to the police station to tell them of the Wanted man and to claim the £100 Reward. At 5p.m. on the evening of Thursday 22nd March Detective Inspector Riding, Detective Sergeant Allan and Detective Idson went to the lodging house of 12 Brunswick Street to take some routine statements from the Landlady and others. It was while the detectives were interviewing the landlady Mrs Bridgewood in the front room that they heard the door opening and the so-called Albert Edwards enter by the kitchen door. Detective Inspector Riding went through to the front room to where Edmonstone was seated. Edmonstone looked up and Detective Riding said to him: "All right Albert" to which Edmonstone replied: "Yes I'm all right" Detective Riding then said "I must warn you that we are detective officers and that anything you say will be written down and can be used in evidence against you...". Edmonstone stood up like a shot and stared coldly at them. Detective Riding then asked: "What do you know of the murder of a young boy in Fifeshire Scotland?" Edmonstone

Dark Skies Over School Wynd

closed his eyes for a few seconds; then as he opened them he suddenly put out his right hand to shake hands with the Detective. "It's all right" he said and threw his hands up in the air in a gesture of submission. The game was up and he knew it. The detectives looked surprised but dealt with Edmunstone immediately ensuring he would not escape. As he was being led away to the police car Edmonstone shook hands with his fellow lodgers, including Atherton. He was heard to say to Mrs Bridgewood "Don't worry about me ma I'll be all right."

The Detectives then took him to the Town Hall and formally charged him with the wilful murder of Michael Swinton Brown at East Wemyss on February 19th, 1909. In reply to the charge Edmonstone said: " I did not know what I was doing."

The Detective then made a search of the man's room where they found a Gladstone bag containing £17 10s in cash wrapped inside personal clothing. Three cash bags which the murdered boy had been carrying were also found along with twenty five £1 bank notes. On Friday 23rd March, almost five weeks after the murder, Edmonstone was brought before the Stipendiary Magistrate at Manchester (Mr Brierly) on a charge of murder and theft. Edmonstone appeared half-dazed as he came into the view of the Court crowded with press men. With his head bowed low and his face flushed, he showed symptoms of nervousness as he stood behind the dock. A telegram had just arrived from the Chief Constable of Fifeshire saying that an escort was on its way to collect the prisoner. Edmonstone was asked if he had any questions? "No Sir", he said feebly.

Dark Skies Over School Wynd

Mr Brierly then asked if he had anything to say? Edmonstone replied: "I did not know what I was doing. My head was a blank." He was then taken to the Town Hall to await the Fife police who would then convey him to Cupar.

Dark Skies Over School Wynd

A Charge of Murder

"Qui percusserit hominem volens occidere morte moriatur."
Exodus XX1 : 12

A large shouting crowd had gathered for the arrival of the murder suspect by car at Cupar. Edmonstone, overcoat buttoned well up to his neck and a green cap drawn well down over his eyes was seated at the back of the car handcuffed between two officers as he was brought back to Scotland to face trial. He ignored the wild cries of "bloody animal" from the growing crowd outside as he walked the short distance to the Court House. Mr G. E. B. Osborne (of Messrs Pagan & Osborne, solicitors) appeared for the prisoner as the charge was read out:

"Your Petitioner is credibly informed that Alexander Edmonstone, Carter, lately residing in East Wemyss did on Friday 19th February 1909 in a public water closet in School Wynd East Wemyss village; (1) rob Michael Swinton Brown, clerk, East Wemyss, of a bag containing £85 of money and of a watch and chain; and (2) did assault Michael Swinton Brown and did seize him by the throat and press it with his (the accused's) hand's and a handkerchief and did kick him on the head and knock his head against a hard object, or strike him on the head with a blunt instrument, fracture his skull and did murder him."

Asked by Sheriff Armour if he wished to make any statement,

Edmonstone replied in a low tone: "I have nothing to say."

Dark Skies Over School Wynd

He was then whisked away to the 'Fair City' of Perth which had been his place of asylum on the night of the murder, only this time as a resident of H.M. Prison. As Edmonstone was led to the car the crowd outside had doubled in size to more than 300. Their number and hostility were growing rapidly and to shouts of "lynch the bastard" the police found it extremely difficult to restrain their attempts to seize hold of Edmonstone only just managing to get him safely inside the car.

The arrival of Edmonstone at Perth Prison had been kept a secret so that when the car holding the prisoner arrived 11.15 a.m. on Monday 27th March no one was at the gate of the Prison except two press men; it was a secret no more after that. Edmonstone was led to solitary confinement in the observation cell No.28 in Division B where he would spend the rest of his time until the date of the trial. This cell was only used when a prisoner was waiting trial on a very grave charge such as murder and a close watch was kept on them day and night.

Meanwhile back in the village of East Wemyss the news of Edmonstone's arrest spread like wildfire amid the clamour for the daily newspapers with the details of his arrest. A solitary policeman still stood outside the small cottage at the East End where the Edmonstone family lived. The news of his arrest after five weeks on the run rekindled the horror of the terrible murder on 19th February and there was now a mixture of relief and excitement in the air. It had also opened old wounds and there was much sympathy for the Brown family who may now have to endure the whole thing in detail through a court trial.

Dark Skies Over School Wynd

Edmonstone was haunted by his own memories of that day when he was asked to wear the clothes he had worn on the 19th February on several occasions for the purpose of witness identification. One by one the witnesses came from all over the country and pointed him out.

Back in the village of East Wemyss on April 5th 1909, the home of William and Helen Brown was in a state of melancholy as the family lamented the day that would have been wee Mickey Brown's sixteenth birthday. All they could do was to place fresh flowers at his grave and remember him fondly.

At a pleading diet in the Procurator Fiscal's Office County Buildings, Perth, on May 28th 1909, Edmonstone pleaded, 'Not Guilty' along with a Special Plea that at the time of the murder he was, 'Insane and not responsible for his actions.'

As a consequence of his lack of funds a 'Defence Fund' to raise money for Edmonstone's agent, Mr Carswell, was put into motion but, understandably, never really got off the ground.

At around 9 o'clock on the morning of Tuesday June 8th 1909, Tay Street in Perth was filling with people all eager to catch a glimpse of Alex Edmonstone, the murder suspect, who was due to appear in front of Lord Guthrie and a jury at the Perth Circuit Court at ten o' clock for the Cause celebre. All available space for the spectators in the Court-room was filled to capacity as they awaited his arrival from the penitentiary. Hundreds of people gathered outside the door of the court and it was with difficulty that ticket holders got inside. Lord Guthrie arrived exactly on time at 10.30 a.m. and within the bar were:- Mr A.M.

Dark Skies Over School Wynd

Anderson; Advocate Deputy and Prosecuting Council; assisted by Mr James Smith, Clark; also Mr J.R. Christie and Mr Napier Armit, Defence Council for Edmonstone and assisted by Mr D Carswell solicitor, Ladybank

At the foot of the gallery there lay a small collection of articles which made up the productions of the case:- The last clothes worn by Mickey Brown; and the garments left by Edmonstone in the lodgings at Renfield Street, Glasgow. The screeching sound of trumpets heralded the start of the proceedings and a Jury was chosen. At 10.15 a.m. to gasps and much excitement in the gallery Edmonstone appeared from below the Court up into the courtroom through a trapdoor accompanied by three policemen. It was noted that there was not the slightest trace of remorse or dejection on his face. On the 'Diet' being called for the Jury to take their seats Edmonstone immediately leapt to his feet thinking that it was the signal for him to stand to account. He was guided back to his seat. On the charge being read out the Clerk said that the prisoner pleaded 'Not Guilty' and a special defence of 'Insanity' was put. Various witnesses were heard from the time of the murder right up to when Edmonstone had been arrested in Manchester. Inspector Peattie of Cupar stated that as he escorted the prisoner home he was very reticent. The prisoner had said however, that he had "intended giving himself up" pointing to his head he had said he "could not stand it any longer." The prisoner's declaration was then read out: It stated that he was 23 years of age, unmarried and was a Carter. He declined to say anything about the case or the charge made against him and this finished the proceedings for the prosecution

Dark Skies Over School Wynd

For the Defence, a painful sensation was created when Mrs Edmonstone, mother of the prisoner, entered the witness box.

A grey-haired and thin-faced weary woman of 49 years of age, Mrs Edmonstone took the oath in wavering tones while her son hung his head and looked down to the floor. Giving a glance at her son in the dock she proceeded to answer the numerous questions put by Mr Christie.

Mrs Edmonstone deponed that, on the morning of the murder, her son had sang his little nephew to sleep with the words, "Just a beautiful picture in a beautiful gilded frame." There was deafening silence as the crowded Court watched the prisoner with tears in his eyes listening to his mother doing her best to save her son from the gallows. In all 43 witnesses were cited for the prosecution and only several for the defence which included medical and mental experts.

On Wednesday 9th June 1909, the second day of the trial Mr Christie, urged that Edmonstone was subject to epileptic fits and that these recurrent seizures had so weakened his intellect that he was not responsible for his actions at the time of the murder. Evidence was led to support this view and the case ultimately turned upon it. Dr J.S. Clouson of Morningside Asylum and Dr L.C. Bruce of Murthly Asylum both 'mental experts' gave their opinion that Edmonstone was labouring under epilepsy. While the symptoms described by the doctors pointed to degeneracy neither of them would go the length of saying that Edmonstone was insane when he committed the murder.

In a clear sign of the times, Lord Guthrie when summing up drew a clear distinction between the mental condition of Edmonstone as shown in the evidence, and that of "men

Dark Skies Over School Wynd

whom boys followed in the street and called a daft so-and-so.", and pointed out that no one claimed that Edmonstone was so insane as to have no responsibility whatsoever at the time of the murder. Lord Guthrie also directed attention to Edmonstone's conduct after his flight from the scene of the crime. As men of the world (it was an all male jury), he asked the jury to judge what took place on 19th February 1909.

They also heard that, in the morning, he did not exhibit any unusual behaviour, and how, prior to 19th February, there was no apparent change in the man's nature. They might put the delirium aside. They would judge what took place immediately before and immediately after the murder. The jury were out for only a few minutes before returning with the awaited verdict. Edmonstone, who had waited impatiently for the return of the jury, pulled himself together and stood erect when the jury gave their unanimous verdict of..." Guilty !" Edmonstone looked stunned as the verdict sank in. He gathered himself again when the Judge pronounced his name. In the hushed courtroom the black cap was placed on the head of Lord Guthrie as he passed the formal sentence:-

"I decern and adjudge you to be carried from the bar to the prison of Perth, therein to be detained till the sixth day of July and on that day between the hours of eight and ten o' clock forenoon within the walls of the said prison, by the hands of the common executioner, to be hanged by the neck on a gibbet till dead, your body thereafter to be buried within the walls of the prison, your moveables and gear to be given over to His Majesty's use. May the lord have mercy on your soul."

Dark Skies Over School Wynd

Edmonstone who had throughout the trial sat stolid like in the dock looked as if he had suddenly been stabbed through the heart by a knife. He sank into the seat in a state of collapse. This judgement had been genuinely unexpected by Edmonstone who had always banked on the plea of Insanity to escape the gallows.

The two police officers on either side of him raised him up and escorted the prisoner down through the trapdoor of Perth Court into the cells below. When conveyed from the Court he showed signs of distress and had to be assisted to the waiting cab after fainting into the arms of the officers.

At the prison gates a large crowd which had assembled caught a glimpse of the prisoner going into the prison and showered him with verbal and physical hostility as he drove past.

As Mrs Edmonstone left Court she was asked for her thoughts on the verdict, she said: "Even when Lord Guthrie was speaking I looked at my son but he never lifted his eyes. For my son to spend his life in prison would be a living death and far worse than death itself. If he was to get a reprieve he would come out a convict and probably find himself motherless, fatherless and penniless and would have nowhere to go. He would again get into the devil's hands. From the time of his arrest in Manchester, Alex confessed his wrong-doing. Our son does not care much for himself, only for us. God help him ! "

McGilvray PRINTERS
Established 1885

Thos. McGilvray & Son Ltd
Wemyss Road Dysart
Kirkcaldy Fife KY1 2XZ
Tel: (01592) 655993 Fax: (01592) 655117
email: sales@mcgilvray.demon.co.uk

Smith & Grant
Solicitors and Estate Agents

Rathellan, High Street, Leven, Fife KY8 4PR

Telephone Leven (01333) 423441   FAX: Leven (01333) 427342

Smith & Grant provides a full legal service to its commercial and personal clients. We have three legal/estate agency offices in Fife and our friendly staff can provide you with any advice which you may require. We undertake all aspects of legal work and estate agency including sale and purchase of property, sales and estates, tax planning, divorce, private companies, industrial tribunals, court work including legal aid, damages and accident claims, employment and commercial law.

WE ARE ALWAYS WILLING TO PREPARE YOUR WILL FREE OF CHARGE

So why not telephone Leven 423441 and make an early appointment.

LET US HELP YOU TODAY

also at 4 Commercial Road, Leven KY8 4LE and 198 Wellesley Road, Methil KY8 3BW

Telephone Leven (01333) 423441   Telephone (01333) 424661
FAX (01333) 427342   FAX (01333) 426660

Wemyss Central Hotel

5 Main Street, East Wemyss
Tel: (01592) 716120   Fax: (01592) 716120

ACCOMMODATION
Three twin rooms suitable for golfing and fishing parties

FUNCTION ROOM
Weddings • Funerals • Private Functions

BAR AND BOAT LOUNGE
*Open 7 days
Meals and Snacks available*

friendly village atmosphere

Learning for Life

KIRKLAND HIGH SCHOOL AND COMMUNITY COLLEGE

wishes

Dominic J. Currie

and

"DARK SKIES OVER SCHOOL WYND"

every success

Have YOU thought about visiting your local Comminity College to find out what is available for you - day or evening? Why not call in to see us at Methil Brae, METHIL, KY7 8LT or phone Mrs Davie on 01333 59 2403.

WE DON'T GO FOR SUDDEN DEATH ...

... but our courses might help you
solve the mysteries of ...

literature, communications, languages, sociology, crafts,
design, health and child care, agriculture,
horticulture, floristry, engineering,
catering, golf greenkeeping...
etc, etc.

Call us on 01334 658800 or
Write FREEPOST, Elmwood, Cupar, KY15 4BR

• FAMILY LAW • PERSONAL LEGAL ADVICE • BUSINESS LAW •

PAGAN OSBORNE

WHERE BEING THE BEST COMES SECOND ONLY TO MEETING YOUR NEEDS

PAGAN OSBORNE LAW CENTRES

• CUPAR •
12 St Catherine St

Tel : 01334 653777

• ST ANDREWS •
83 Market Street

Tel : 01334 475001

• DUNDEE •
45 Reform Street

Tel : 01382 314800

• ANSTRUTHER •
15 East Shore

Tel : 01333 310703

PAGAN OSBORNE PROPERTY CENTRES

• CUPAR •
1 Crossgate

Tel : 01334 656525

• ST ANDREWS •
9 Church Street

Tel : 01334 475151

• ANSTRUTHER •
15 East Shore

Tel : 01333 310703

PAGAN MACBETH BUSINESS LAW

• CUPAR •
12 St Catherine Street

Tel : 01334 657000

• EDINBURGH •
8 Manor Place

Tel : 0131 220 3334

• DUNFERMLINE •
38 High Street

Tel : 01383 731011

An Investment in Peace of Mind

• INVESTMENT MANAGEMENT • LICENSING • CONVEYANCING •

Solve your training needs...

choose Lauder

for

- vocational and leisure courses
- education and training on a full-time, part-time or flexible basis
- HNC and HND courses with possible direct entry onto 2nd or 3rd year of a university college degree course

Tel 01383 845010

Halbeath, Dunfermline,
Fife KY11 5DY

Promoting Excellence in Education and Training

PLAN YOUR
future

AT FIFE COLLEGE KIRKCALDY

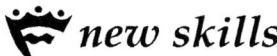 new skills

 new opportunties

 new qualifications

Where can you go to choose from one of the widest range of Further and Higher Education programmes available in Scotland?

Fife College in Kirkcaldy - offers qualifications from National Certificate to Higher National Certificate/Diploma to Degree level and beyond, covering a wide variety of subject areas.

Whatever your choice for the future - take your first step to a successful career by making Fife College your next stop.

For further information contact:
The Access Information Unit
Fife College of Further and Higher Education,
St. Brycedale Avenue,
Kirkcaldy, Fife KY1 1EX.
or FREEPHONE

0800 413280

FAX: (01592) 640225

Fife College
of Further and Higher Education

FIFE COLLEGE EXISTS TO PROMOTE AND
EXTEND THE QUALITY OF EDUCATION
THROUGHOUT THE COMMUNITY

GIVE ME FIFE!

EUROPEAN SOCIAL FUND GB

Dark Skies Over School Wynd

Sentence of Death

Edmonstone maintained a condition of absolute dejection for some days, but seemed resigned to his fate after receiving offers of kind ministrations from Rev W.E. Lee. of the East Parish Church Perth. In a letter to his father, he stated that he had made his peace with god and referred his parents to god for strength in the coming days. Neither of Edmonstone's parents made any effort to gain a reprieve for their son feeling that it would be hopeless to look for support for such a petition and so left it to Mr Carswell.

Arrangements for the execution of Edmonstone on Tuesday 6th July 1909 rested with the Magistrates of Perth. It was to be on the Monday but the 5th of July was a holiday for the executioner so it was changed to the Tuesday. Bailies Lawrie and Forrest, the two Junior Magistrates, were appointed to see the warrant carried into effect. John Ellis, the famous number one hangman (1901 - 1924), was appointed as the executioner.

Mr John Begg the town clerk was instructed to communicate with the Glasgow corporation with a view to getting the use of the scaffold which was erected there recently.

In the streets of Perth, Rev R.S. Barclay of St Mark's Chapel was appealing to the public to sign a petition for a reprieve from the sentence of death placed upon Edmonstone. Contained within the petition were several reasons for their rejections of the death sentence. These were: 'That the prisoner was labouring from serious disease of the brain. Also that because there were no funds to meet the expense of a proper defence the prisoner was prohibited from bringing forward other medical witnesses who may have been prepared to state that he was insane and not responsible for his actions at the time of the crime.

That the prisoner was only 23 years of age, and, up until the day of the tragedy had borne a good character. The petition asked the Secretary of State for Scotland, Lord Pentland, to exercise his Royal prerogative to commute the death sentence.

Edmonstone passed away his final days on earth by writing copious letters to his family. One of them pleaded with his parents: "I hope you are not always thinking of me as one who has blackened your name and the name I bear" and, in a closing address, he states: "I think I will close, dear mother, as my head is likely to break down when I think of all the sorrow I have brought on you."

Guilty of a shocking and disgusting crime, it may well have been the shame of his actions which weighed so heavily on his conscience that made him decide not to fight for his life or even expect any commutation of the death sentence. As a gambler, Edmonstone was well aware of the high stakes on February 19th and, for a while his luck held. He also came to accept the death sentence passed on himself perhaps because of his real fears of a long and confined prison sentence and all the consequences that came with the label of being a child murderer even in 1909.

It was not uncommon for a kind of friendship to develop and for the condemned cell duty men to become sympathetic to the prisoner. In this case however, this did not happen, though Edmonstone did ask the guards a great deal of questions: 'Where is the gallows?' 'Does it take

Dark Skies Over School Wynd

long?' 'Will it hurt?'. The advice he received was grim but helpful: "If you have to go, it's better if you go quietly and quickly. It's better for you and it's better for everybody."

On Saturday 4th of July Edmonstone was lying on his bed when he heard footsteps stopping outside his cell. The door of his cell was swung open.

Mr Jas Turpie, Town Clerk, and the Governor, Mr James Grant, delivered the answer to the appeal for the commutation of death from the Secretary of Scotland, Lord Pentland.

It read:-

"Dear Sir - With reference to the case of Alexander Edmonstone, now lying under sentence of death at His Majesty's Prison Perth, I have to inform you that after careful consideration, I regret that I am unable to discover sufficient grounds to justify me in advising His Majesty to interfere with the due course of the law.

I am, Sir, Your obedient servant,"

Lord Pentland.

Edmonstone received the news with dejection and deathly silence. It was evident that he fully understood the contents of the letter which had now sealed his fate.

Dark Skies Over School Wynd

Brunswick Street in Manchester where Edmonstone left every morning for his so-called 'work' at a nearby Motor Show.

The end of the road for the Wemyss Murderer. The lodgings of Mrs Bridgewood was here in Brunswick Street where Edmonstone kept the stolen money hidden under the bed inside a gladstone bag. His days were numbered when the peddlar John Atherton moved into the same lodgings.

Dark Skies Over School Wynd

Outside Whitworth Police Station in Manchester: circa 1909. Edmonstone gave himself up to the Manchester Detectives. While inside the car he kept repeating; "I didn't know what I was doing; my mind was a blank".

The old Entrance to Perth Prison where crowds of thousands awaited the hoisting of the black flag that would signal the execution of the Wemyss Murderer. Edmonstone's remains still lie buried within the walls of the prison.

Dark Skies Over School Wynd

Perth High Court on Tay Street where Lord Guthrie sentenced Edmonstone to death. During the trial hundreds of people thronged the entrance hoping to gain access to the trial. Following his sentence he was taken to the cells below to await transport for the short journey to Perth Prison.

The lone figure of the prisoner stands before the judge amid the sombre surroundings of Perth High Court (1909) while the charge (of murder) is read out. Edmonstone's plea of 'not guilty' with a special plea of 'Insanity at the time of the murder' cut no ice with the jury who returned a verdict of guilty without any recommendation of mercy.

Dark Skies Over School Wynd

Lord Guthrie: Pencilled sketch of the famous judge who reminded the jury that they needed to consider the crime in the light of a lack of any evidence of insanity before and after the murder. There was only one sentence that was ever going to satisfy the horrified and disgusted public - Death by hanging.

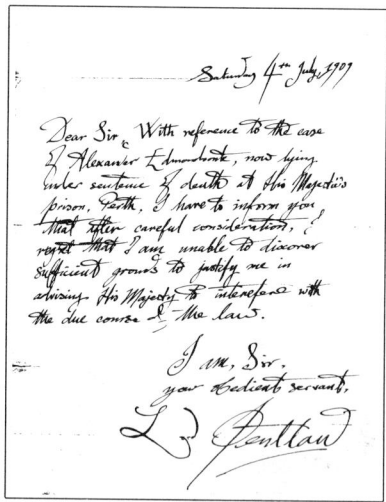

The letter which sealed Edmonstone's fate for all time. From now on he was doomed at the hands of the Public Executioner.

Dark Skies Over School Wynd

The Sepulchre Bell

Edmonstone, in the condemned cell you lie,
Prepare well; for tomorrow you must die:
Watch all and pray. The hour is drawing near.
Where you before Almighty must appear.

Examine well yourself; in time repent.
That you may not to that eternal hell be sent.
And when the Sepulchre Bell at dawn does toll.
May the Lord above have mercy on your soul.

Anonymous 1909

On Tuesday 6th July a large crowd of over a thousand people congregated outside the gates of Perth Prison to witness the hoisting of the black flag which would announce the death of the Wemyss murderer. Although the execution was timed to take place at eight o' clock many people began to gather at seven a.m. to witness the simple ceremony. A detachment of Police officers was stationed at the entrance to the prison and no one was admitted beyond the Prison gate other than the officials and five representatives of the press. Inside the prison, Edmonstone had been up since three o' clock in the morning nervously awaiting the arrival of Rev W.E. Lee in the cell he had occupied since sentence was passed upon him.

Inside the cell was a single bed under a barred window, a table and a few chairs, all simple and basic. The two lonely men sat by the window in prayer. A short distance away the scaffold had been tested the previous day with a bag of sand the same weight as Edmonstone by Ellis the executioner

Dark Skies Over School Wynd

and found it to be in perfect working order. At six o' clock Edmonstone was moved to the cell adjoining the execution chamber at the north wall of the prison and sat down to a hearty breakfast. The execution chamber itself had been an old brick store of about 12 feet square which had been converted for these very occasions.

At a few minutes to eight o' clock Edmonstone could hear the steady tread of the approaching execution party.

As Edmonstone walked his last few steps along the prison yard to the execution chamber he ascended the short stair leading to the upper floor where the scaffold was erected. His face as white as marble as the town clock began to chime for eight o' clock.

When the procession reached the scaffold the condemned man faltered slightly as he caught sight of the great dark beam over the centre of the room and a white rope hanging from the centre down to head height above a large trap-door. He was handed over to Ellis the executioner who was now responsible for carrying out the sentence of death. Baillie Lawrie asked the prisoner if he desired to make any statement? No statement was made. Neither did he make any attempt to deny his guilt. He simply thanked the officers for their kindness and said, "I have nothing more to say." Ellis the executioner quickly secured his arms lightly with a strap and as Edmonstone steadily walked the few remaining yards to the scaffold the Rev W.E. Lee walked behind him reading the funeral service while the Magistrates and officials took their places and moved off to the scaffold. Edmonstone's manner and self control was cool calm and collected as he stopped at the chalk mark on the trapdoor. Ellis pulled the white bag over

Dark Skies Over School Wynd

the unresisting Carter's head (traditionally to give the condemned man some dignity in death). Edmonstone was heard to repeat after the chaplain's prayer, "The Lord have mercy on my soul." He then pulled the rope down over his neck securing the knot tightly under his left jaw and instantly make for the lever. The executioner pulled down the lever and Edmonstone disappeared seven feet into the darkened pit quickly followed by a loud sharp click as the rope parted his second and third vertebrae and broke his neck.

Death was instantaneous for Alexander Edmonstone who had now become the last prisoner ever to be hanged at Perth Prison.

Outside hundreds more had gathered on the Craigie Bridge and as the black flag was hoisted up the prison flagpole the crowd behaved with a mixture of silence and wild emotions. Sheriff Sym made an official inspection of the body shortly after nine o' clock where it was then removed and buried in a newly dug grave beside the north wall of the Prison. The only memorial being the letters "A.E. 1909" carved into the adjoining wall.

It was clean, efficient and very quick.

The final few chimes of the town clock outside had just sounded for eight o' clock as the last chapter of the Wemyss Murder came to a close.

Dark Skies Over School Wynd

Looking down School Wynd. It hasn't changed much since the day of the murder. To the left is the East Wemyss primary school where Mickey Brown did so well. The road veers off to the right at the trees where the fateful public lavatory is still there to this day.

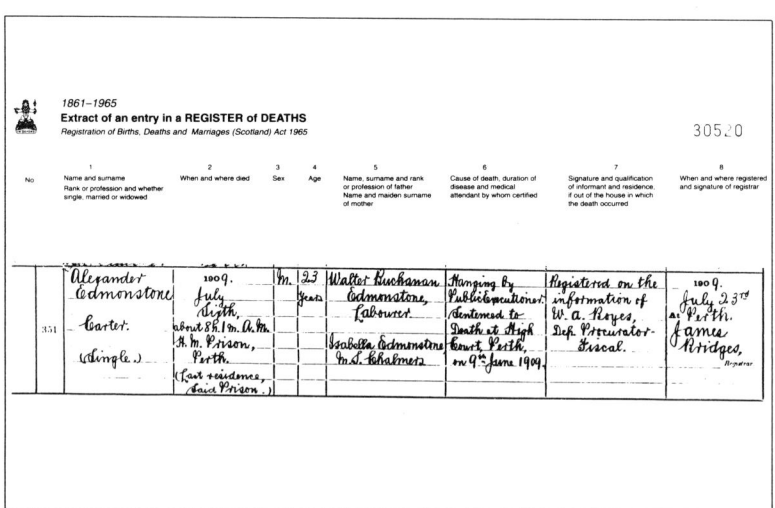

The final formality and the last piece of material connected with the Ex-Carter from Wemyss. The Death Certificate of Alexander Emonstone showing that death was by Hanging by the Public Executioner.

Dark Skies Over School Wynd

No	Name and Surname Rank or profession and whether single, married or widowed	When and where died	Sex	Age	Name, surname and rank or profession of father Name and maiden surname of mother	Cause of death, duration of disease, and medical attendant by whom certified	Signature and qualification of informant, and residence, if out of the house in which the death occurred	When and where registered and signature of registrar
15	Michael Swinton BROWN Linen Manufacturer's Clerk (Apprentice) (Single)	1909 February Nineteenth About 0h 30m p.m. in Public Lavatory School Wynd East Wemyss U.R. Parkhill Terrace East Wemyss	M	15 years	William Brown Mason Journeyman Helen Brown m.s. Swinton	Probable cause of Death Haemorrhage Shock (Seen after death) As Cert. by Robert Balfour Graham F.R.C.S. D.P.H.R.	Signed William Brown Father Parkhill Terrace East Wemyss	1909 February 20th At East Wemyss Signed David Laing Reg

The Death Certificate of Michael Swinton Brown showing the Cause of Death to be 'Probable' Haemorrhage and shock although the Post Mortem elaborated by stating death was caused by aggravated attempts at Strangulation produced by external violence.

L to R: Alex Johnston (90) nephew of Mickey Brown. Mickey held Alex as a new born infant in 1908 and bought him a small toy dog. Bella Cormie (96) remembers running from her home in Coaltown of Wemyss to the scene of the murder with her sister on Friday 19th 1909. Dom Currie author, standing at the monument to Michael Brown and family in Wemyss cemetery.

Dark Skies Over School Wynd

Another view of the fateful lavatory from the opposite side. Taken in Feb 1909

The forbidding little public lavatory looking down School Wynd as it looks today (1998). It was re-built after the war but was bricked up in the late 1960's.

Dark Skies Over School Wynd

John Ellis the U.K. no.1 executioner from 1901-1924 was appointed to carry out the hanging of Alex Edmonstone. Ironically, Ellis himself went mad and took his own life, cutting his own throat with a razor.

The east end of East Wemyss where the murderer Edmonstone lived with his parents. The houses over looked by the Wemyss cemetery where Mickey Brown is laid to rest.

Dark Skies Over School Wynd

The murder of Mickey Brown raised a national outcry and almost every national newspaper covered the story: This is just a small example.

Dark Skies Over School Wynd

Memento-mori

As with all tragedies, it ends in death. Today when wages are transported from a bank to a place of work the security is understandably tight and very safety conscious. Not so in 1909. It was never part of the social landscape to waste time on hypothetical improbabilities. Hanging was a part of the social landscape and thoughts of 'no one would ever dare do such a thing' were a part of the Victorian business and social culture. The conditions for such a tragedy as the East Wemyss murder were all in place; it only needed the character of a man like Edmonstone to complete such a disastrous calamity. He had a very weak and feeble mind. Short of a plea for mental disorder there still remained the strong possibility of a real link between his general level of emotional instability and his murderous behaviour on Black Friday. A person whose emotions are subject to rapid swings or changes of mood but who is not so seriously disturbed as to be regarded as suffering from insanity can often be described as 'emotionally liable.' Some criminologists today have connected this state with serious criminal behaviour. On Friday, February 19th 1909 opportunity created the conditions for a 'pre-meditated' murder and robbery to take place. It was a disaster waiting to happen. As a result one family was left to hold the shattered remnants of a life without their proud and promising son cut down with all his best years still in front of him.

The murder left behind one little photograph of Mickey; a few school notes; a watch and chain; a few often-repeated

Dark Skies Over School Wynd

stories and an emptiness that steadily compounded itself over the years.

The Brown's were a different family after the murder. Something had gone from their heart never to be replaced.

Tears welled up in eyes at unexpected moments and the family became defined by those who were absent from it.

In the village of Wemyss a cloud of melancholy hung over the place for many years after the murder. A long trial period of time would pass before strangers would be so readily accepted into the village again. As for the Edmonstone family they were eventually forced to change their name and move out of the quiet and peaceful village they had called home since their arrival in 1902. Such was the burden of their shame.

The village of East Wemyss became a much visited spectacle for the macabre and the curious. The Wemyss people tried hard to put the tragedy behind them but it was never to be forgotten. They longed for the mundane during their months of extraordinary social and mental torment and for many years after generations of children were brought up to be always very careful and suspicious when strangers were about.

Though it is through such stories as the Wemyss Murder, that folk lore and nightmares are made.

I here now close the story with this thought.

It is in vain to torment oneself over sufferings from a tragedy which happened so very long ago. However, we can learn from it. If the Wemyss Murder teaches us anything it is that we have a collective responsibility to those in weak and vulnerable positions. Not just to lament a loss but to prevent one. The injustice of sending vulnerable youngsters

Dark Skies Over School Wynd

on missions of death did not end with the murder of Michael Brown. If only it had. We are swift to punish the guilty, but far too slow to clear the danger from the innocent. We must never allow this to happen again.

If we can learn these lessons then Michael Brown's death will not have been in vain.

THE END

Dark Skies Over School Wynd

ABOUT THE AUTHOR

Dominic Currie is a graduate of Fife College gaining a Diploma in Communication Studies and is currently working as a Tutor with Lauder College in Dunfermline. Besides publishing various articles, he is the author of 'The Free Newspapers' 1992; 'A History of The Curries' and 'The Methil Maverick'. He is vice chairman of the Fife Mining Heritage Society and currently doing research on the Michael Colliery and a history of Lauder College.

Dominic also writes poetry, some of which have gained national recognition. He lives in East Wemyss and is married with two children.

7072245R00055

Printed in Great Britain
by Amazon.co.uk, Ltd.,
Marston Gate.

Conclusion

Thanks for buying and reading this book. I hope you have enjoyed the tips and ideas contained in this book, and that they have helped you save time and money, and made everyday tasks a little easier for you.

If you enjoyed this book and would like to share your thoughts with others, please take a moment to write a review on Amazon. It would be much appreciated ☺

Best wishes!

Naya

Connect with Naya Lizardo

Amazon Author Page: http://amzn.to/10T8oQD

Blog: http://forvibranthealth.wordpress.com

Twitter: http://Twitter.com/nayalizardo

mouth of the plunger over the dented area and move it around a little until it seals. Pump the plunger a few times to make sure it's sealed properly and to create good suction. Give the handle a sharp tug. This should pop the metal into its original place. If you are not successful the first time, repeat the process.

Shift into Neutral

To make life for your engine a little easier, shift into neutral when waiting at traffic lights. This technique reduces the amount of heat carried by the cooling system and can increase gas mileage a bit.

Turn on the Heat to Cool Your Engine

Although it is less common with newer cars, even well maintained vehicles can overheat in the right conditions. If your car begins to overheat, the first thing you need to do is turn off the air conditioner and open the windows. Then turn the heater and blower on. Although you'll be really hot, your engine will begin to cool because the heat will be transferred from the engine to the passenger cabin.

Lighten Up Your Key Chain

If your key chain has a dozen keys on it, the weight of the heavy keychain hanging on the ignition, combined with bouncing when you drive, can wear out the tumblers inside the ignition and eventually lead to ignition switch failure. To prevent this from happening, purchase a lightweight key chain that allows you to separate your ignition key from the others. Drive with only the ignition key in your ignition.

Protect Car Door from Garage Walls

If you have a small garage, you might have dinged your car door a time or two by hitting it against the wall. You can prevent this in the future by cutting a pool noodle in half and affixing it horizontally to the wall where the door usually impacts the wall when you open it. The noodle will cushion the impact and prevent damage to your car door.

Remove Car Dent with a Plunger

Taking your car to a mechanic, even for a small dent, can be expensive. Some smooth small to medium sized dents can be removed easily with a regular household plunger (creased or complex dents cannot be removed this way). First rinse and clean the dented area well. Firmly attach the

Your engine has to work harder when there is reduced airflow. Check the filter when you change your oil and replace it at least once a year.

Get Unstuck

Place a bag of kitty litter in your trunk in case you get stuck in snow. If you do get stuck, sprinkle some under the tires to help them get traction.

Ice-Proof Your Car Windows

Do you hate waking up early in the morning to scrape the ice off your car windows? To avoid having to do this, fill a spray bottle with three parts vinegar to one part water, and spray on your car windows on cold winter nights. Vinegar contains acetic acid, which prevents water from freezing. When you wake up in the morning, your car windows should be free of that hateful icy mess. You can also just spray the mixture directly on the icy windows and watch the ice melt.

Keep Rain off Windshields

Sprinkle some baking soda on a damp cloth and wipe your windshield with it. This will create an invisible shield that will make the raindrops bead and roll off.

Clear Up Foggy Headlights

If your headlights are looking little foggy, use toothpaste to remove the grime. Apply regular plain toothpaste (not mint gel or extra-whitening paste) with a soft cloth and rub them using circular motion. Rinse the paste off with water and wipe with a clean cloth.

Extend the Life of Wipers

If wipers are beginning to wear down, you can extend their life by rubbing them briskly with sandpaper.

Fix Fine Scratches with Nail Polish

Even small scratches on your car can be quite annoying. Fixing small scratches doesn't have to require expensive bodywork. You can easily fix small chips and fine scratches with nail polish. First wash and dry the area well. Nail polish is a lacquer and can be used over small car scratches to help cover them and prevent them from rusting. Clear polish won't hide the damage, but it will stop it from getting worse.

Get Better Gas Mileage

Improve your gas mileage by changing your air filter regularly. Your engine sucks in about 14 million gallons of air through the filter every year.

10. Car Tips and Solutions

Avoid the Gasoline Tanker

If you happen to see a gasoline tanker filling the tanks at your local gas station, fill up elsewhere or come back another day. As the station's tanks are being filled, the turbulence can stir up sediment. Sediment in your gas tank can clog fuel filters and fuel injectors, causing poor performance and possibly the need for repairs.

way once and for all, so you can tackle your real emails. Use the filter function and search "unsubscribe", this will bring up all the marketing emails, you'll then be able delete all or drag them all into a separate folder so you can deal with them later. This will drastically reduce the time you spend sifting through your inbox to find important emails you actually need to read and address.

Turn Off Instant Messaging

Instant messaging technology is fantastic, but it makes it too easy to be interrupted and interruptions kill productivity. If someone really needs to reach you, they can call, text or email you.

Work Offline

You'll be amazed at how much work you get done if you disconnect your Internet connection for a few hours each day. When you do go online, do it for a predetermined amount of time. You will be surprised how productive you can be when you are not being constantly interrupted by emails or distracted by surfing the net or checking blogs and newsletters.

Learn to Single-Task

To improve your productivity, learn to focus on one task at a time. Many of us believe that multi-tasking is something we should strive for, but in reality, it often makes you less efficient because of the need to switch gears for each new task, and then switch back again.

Listen To Audio Books

Are you always beating yourself up for not reading enough? Get more reading done by listening to your books while driving, doing laundry, or washing dishes. It will make those tasks less dull and tedious and might even make you smarter.

Put Yourself in Airplane Mode

Many people find that they can be quite productive during airplane flights. For a few hours, you are away from common distractions like coworkers, TV, email, phone, text messaging, and time-sucking web sites. For more productivity, spend a few hours each day in airplane mode: disable the Internet on your computer and put your phone in airplane mode.

Reduce Inbox Clutter

If your inbox is cluttered with spam and your important emails are becoming lost in the shuffle, you'll want to delete or move the spam out of the

9. Productivity Solutions

We all need a productivity boost now and then. Try these excellent productivity tricks to help you be more productive and accomplish more in less time so you have more time to do the things you enjoy most.

Avoid Perfectionism

It is good to use perfection as a guide, but you must also accept that absolute perfection is unattainable. Perfectionism can inflate your workload and cause you to sink time into work well past the point of diminishing returns. That is time you could have spent working on your next task.

you frequent a dry cleaner that does alternations, they'll probably do it for free.

Compare Prices

You don't have to buy an item from the first online site you find. If you're serious about saving money, take the time to shop around and compare prices. You don't have to spend hours comparison-shopping, just check your favorite online shopping sites or sellers for that "perfect" price.

Keep an Eye out Sales

Most online retailers consistently have sales or present promotional offers once or twice a month. The key to taking advantage of sales on some of your favorite clothing items is to try to find out when they typically have them so you can cash in; this will take a bit of tracking to notice a trend but your efforts will pay off.

Read Customer Reviews and Testimonials

Reading customer reviews and/or testimonials is a big deal. You should read both the highest and lowest ratings, and only order from businesses that consistently have the highest rating. You'll also want to check out how many transactions they've actually had. The higher the number of transactions, the more confident you can be about your order.

Fortunately, many online retailers offer free shipping, if the minimum purchase amount is met. There are also many reputable online retailers that charge reasonable shipping fees, so just keep an eye out for those.

What's the Return Policy

Make sure to leave yourself a way out if you end up not being satisfied with the clothing you ordered whether it's because it doesn't fit, isn't as advertised, or you simply aren't thrilled with it. Most online retailers offer a written return policy, but you want to make sure it doesn't have any unseen loopholes. Look for sellers that offer hassle free returns. If you don't see a return policy listed, email the seller before buying and be sure to save their response if they say they have one.

Know Your Size and Measurements

Shopping for clothes online can get you fantastic designer brands and styles at bargain prices. However, it also comes with pitfalls because you're buying a clothing item without trying it on first. Sure, if you ordered from a seller that has a good return policy, you can always send it back, but that comes with the hassle of repackaging and returning it and taking the time to return it. Once you have an idea of your size, you'll be able shop stress free. You may even want to go to a tailor to make sure you have the right measurements and if

8. Online Shopping Tips

Most of us today do at least a little online shopping. It's convenient, fast, and for the most part, easy, if you know how to do to it efficiently. With a little time and foresight, you'll be able to find great prices, ensure your items fit once they arrive and have fun doing it. The following tips will help you have successful online transactions every time you shop.

Know the Delivery Costs

What initially may seem like a great deal can quickly end up in disappointment once you add in the shipping costs and fees that, in many cases, end up being more than the cost of the item itself.

your pocket. The sheet will act as a mosquito repellent and will even make you smell fresher as you walk or hike.

Learn Some Local Language

When traveling abroad, a few words and phrases in the local language will go a long way to make your trip more pleasant. You may need them to talk to locals who don't know your language. Or you may simply want to use them to impress the people there. At a bare minimum, you should learn: "Please", "Thank you", "Yes", "No", "Excuse me", "Restroom", "One", and "Two."

Tip Sooner

If you are in the good habit of tipping your hotel staff, try introducing yourself to the staff and giving them a small tip at the beginning of your stay. You will likely get a few more chocolates on your pillow, extra coffee packets, and fresh towels.

loose bills in case someone robs or pick pockets you.

Don't Lose Your Travel Companion

If you are traveling abroad with a companion, especially in a busy city, be sure pick a central location to meet up in case you become separated. Nothing is more stressful and anxiety inducing than losing your travel companion in strange city, not having a working cell phone and not knowing how or where to meet up.

Email Your Itinerary to Yourself

Email your flight, hotel reservation and other confirmation numbers to yourself. Also, email yourself copies of your passport. If your bags are lost or stolen, you'll be able to retrieve this information from any Internet café.

Have a Day with No Plans

Carefully planning your trip is a good idea, however, you should also keep a day open to chill out or walk around without any particular destination in mind. It's simply relaxing.

Keep Mosquitoes Away

When hiking in the mountains or touring around that idyllic Caribbean island, mosquitos are a given. To keep them away, place a dryer sheet in

Enjoy Your Trip More

Vacations are wonderful times to rejuvenate and restore your soul and body, and there are simple things you can do to help ensure you can enjoy your vacation to the fullest.

Avoid Being a Target

To avoid being a target of crime, do not wear conspicuous clothing or jewelry and do not carry excessive amounts of cash. Consider carrying a decoy wallet with cancelled credit cards and a few already know that you can't take liquids in containers larger than 3 ounces on your carry-on luggage. Make sure to pack your liquids in your checked luggage to avoid delays when going through security. Also, remember not to wrap gifts before you travel. Packages that are gift-wrapped can't be easily identified and security officials will likely have to unwrap them, causing you more delays.

Minimize the Risk of Problems

Try to book tickets with as few stops as possible. Each layover increases the chances of missed flights, delays and lost luggage. Also, avoid booking layover stops through cities that have a good chance of weather related delays like Chicago in the winter.

Travel with Recognizable Luggage

If possible, choose luggage you can easily recognize. If your luggage is black or brown luggage, be sure to affix something colorful on it like a bright label or a ribbon so you can easily spot your bag. You can also purchase colored handle straps for a sleeker look.

Check-In Online

Most airlines allow passengers to check in up to 24 hours in advance, select seat assignments, and print boarding passes. Do this in advance to avoid having to wait in lengthy airport check-in lines. If you travel with only carry-on bags, you can go straight to security at the airport.

Check Bags at Curbside

If you must check bags, you shouldn't hesitate to use the curbside baggage check service offered by most airlines. The usual tip of $1 per bag will spare you a good deal of aggravation and time. By using curbside baggage check-in, you can avoid the long lines at the front desk and go straight to your gate to check in.

Easily Swap Seats

If you are traveling with someone, but your travel companion can't get an adjacent seat, get an aisle seat as far forward as possible. Once everyone is seated, you can ask the person traveling next to your travel companion to swap with you. The forward aisle seats have the highest value for trading with other passengers.

Follow Packing Rules

Know your airline's weight and size restrictions for carry-ons and checked bags. Most people to avoid the risk of lost luggage. Sometimes however, checking your bags is necessary. If you must check bags, avoid flashy high-end luggage. If thieves are out to steal a piece of luggage, it will likely be one these. Although bags are stolen at airports, the main reason bags are lost is because they were routed to the wrong destination. Be sure to remove old airline destination tags to prevent this from happening.

Carry a Power Splitter

Many airports now provide power outlets or charging stations for your phone or computers. If you are stuck waiting around at the airport and your phone or computer battery is running low, this can be a lifesaver. Often, however (especially during peak travel times), when you need one most, all the outlets are already taken. Take a small power splitter with you, and ask someone if you can share the outlet by using the splitter. Most people would agree to do so.

Dress for Security

New regulations require that you take off your shoes before going through security, but you might also be asked to take off your coat or sweater, belt, jewelry, and any other items containing metal. To avoid unnecessary delays, wear easily removable shoes and remove your jacket and sweater beforehand.

Breeze Through the Airport

The idea of frazzled nerves, long lines, and lengthy delays at the airport make many travelers shudder. To make your trip to the airport less painful, try these timesaving tips that will help you avoid the usual airport hassles.

Avoid Lost Luggage

Most savvy travelers avoid checking bags for several reasons. One is to avoid the hassles of waiting around at baggage claim and the other is

Use TSA Approved Locks

If you want to lock your luggage, be sure to use a TSA-approved one. The TSA reserves the right to access all luggage, so if you use a regular lock for your suitcase, it might be gone when you get your luggage back.

Pack a Sarong

Sarongs are lightweight and incredibly versatile so be sure to pack one. You can use it as a bathing suit cover, airplane blanket, picnic blanket, and tablecloth, or even as an emergency towel.

Pack a Shoe Organizer for More Storage

Go to the dollar store and find yourself an over the door shoe organizer. You want a plastic or mesh one. Hang this on the bathroom door in your hotel room or cruise cabin and you'll have tons of pockets for things like toiletries, air freshener, shoes, belts, and more.

Shower Cap Shoe Bag

When traveling, use a disposable shower cap as shoe bag. The shower cap will cover the dirty soles of your shoes and keep them from dirtying the clothes in your suitcase. They take up very little room and are easy and convenient to put on and take off.

Split Up Your Stuff

If you are not traveling alone, it's a great idea to pack some of your stuff in your travel companion's bag and vice versa. That way, if your bag or your companion's bag is lost, you will each still have some clothing.

Keep Silk Scarves from Wrinkling

Wrap your silk scarves around an empty roll of paper towel. This will keep them from wrinkling. Keep it in place by putting a rubber band on each end.

Keep Powder Make-Up from Breaking

To keep your pressed powder make-up from cracking or breaking when you travel, place a round cotton pad on top and close the lid. The cotton will serve as cushion, protecting the powder.

Pack All Liquids in a Ziploc Bag

Pack all your liquids containers in 1 gallon size Ziploc bags. You never know when a bottle of conditioner, body lotion, or sunblock will open and the Ziploc bag will keep your clothes from being ruined.

Pack a Doorstop

If you are traveling alone to a less than idyllic location and want to feel extra safe when you sleep, wedge a rubber doorstop on the inside of the hotel door and the door will be almost impossible to open from the outside.

Packing Tips and Ideas

Carry a Silk Travel Blanket for the Plane

Bringing a warm blanket on planes is a good idea, but regular blankets can be bulky. Silk blankets are as warm as regular blankets, but take up far less space. Silk also has incredible temperature regulating properties, keeping you warm when the weather is chilly and cool when the weather is warmer.

great savings. TripAlertz.com works a little bit like Groupon for travel, the more people who book a deal, the lower the rate.

Save On Your Next Cruise

To save money on your next cruise, you might want to consider booking your next cruise when onboard. Some cruise lines offer significant discounts if you book your next cruise while on your current cruise.

Use a Different Credit Card

When you use your credit card or bankcard abroad, many American banks charge a foreign transaction fee of around 3%. If you withdraw cash from ATM, you will also likely be charged an ATM withdrawal fee by the foreign bank and by your own bank. It adds up quickly. There are a few exceptions, Capital One for example, does not charge a foreign transaction fee, and depending on your type of account, will credit back any ATM fees charged by other banks.

are considered the worst day. This is when the airlines test higher fares in the hopes that competitors will match the high fares.

Rack Up the Miles

If you want to rack up miles, consider booking flights that have multiple legs. These are usually much cheaper, yet they can earn a lot more miles and get you closer to frequent flyer status. You can easily rack up 20-30% more miles this way.

Save on Baggage Fees

The best thing to do to save on baggage fees is to pack light. But if you absolutely can't pack light, then I suggest you pack more bags. Yes, pack more bags! It's cheaper to pay for a second bag than to pay the fee for one overweight bag. Most major domestic carriers charge around $25 for the first bag and $35 for second. That is $60; it's not cheap, but if you only bring one bag and exceed the limit by a few pounds, you will either have to throw out some of your clothes to lighten the load or pay at a minimum $90 for the overweight fee.

Save By Shopping Private Sales

Many new websites, including SniqueAway.com, TabletHotels.com, and Jetsetter.com, offer invitation-only flash sales that give you 20% to 60% off hotel packages to travelers. Livingsocial.com offers last-minute getaways at

Pay Lower Hotel Prices

When you make a hotel reservation, it pays to ask the front desk for a lower rate. Always ask, "Is this the lowest price you have?" Many times, they will be able find you a lower price or offer you an additional discount.

Pay Less for Taxis

When you arrive at your destination, you will likely see a line of taxis waiting to take passengers to the city center. Avoid taking these taxis, which are often charged airport surcharge to wait for passengers, which they will pass on to their passengers. Instead, head over to the departure area of the airport and wait for a taxi dropping customers off.

Purchase Packages

You can often save by purchasing a hotel and airline package, even if you don't plan on using the hotel portion. Many times, the combined airline and hotel price is lower than the airline price alone.

Purchase Ticket at the Right Time

Many travel experts agree that early Wednesday morning is the best time to purchase tickets. Try purchasing your tickets just after midnight when the new fares have been freshly uploaded. Fridays

Money Saving Tips and Ideas

Get Bumped Off Your Flight

Many people dread the possibility of being bumped from their flight because it's over sold. Getting bumped from a flight isn't always a bad thing. If you are willing to put up with some waiting around and other inconveniences, it can lead to big rewards. If an airline is oversold and they ask volunteers to take a later flight in exchange for a $400 travel voucher, being bumped can really pay. To improve your chances of being bumped off your next flight, try booking during the busiest business hours, as airlines will often oversell flights during prime business hours. Be sure to add yourself to the volunteer list early.

friends. It's no wonder traveling is such a popular thing to do!

If, after months of scrimping and saving, you are now planning that long awaited vacation, this section will provide you with some handy tips and ideas that are sure to make your travels more pleasant and fun. These tips and tricks will help you make the most of your experience and save a little cash while you're at it so you can then use it on something much more fun, like a few extra margaritas or rumrunners on the beach!

7. Travel Hints and Tips

Vacations can really bring you long lasting joy and happiness. The happiness starts from the moment the idea popped into your head; from that moment, you feel a wonderful sense of anticipation. The excitement builds as you plan the details of your trip and then there's the joy and exhilaration you feel once you're on vacation. It's bliss! And the sense of joy lasts even after you return home from vacation as you relive your trip and share the happy moments with family and skin affected by sunburns and irritants like poison ivy.

Gargle with Whiskey for a Sore Throat

Add a spoonful of whiskey and a teaspoon of honey to warm water and gargle; the whiskey will help numb the throat and the honey will help coat the throat and soothe irritation.

Keep the Bugs Away with Homemade Insect Repellent

Insects carry a variety of dangerous diseases, so it's a good idea to keep them as far away from you as possible. You can make your own natural and inexpensive bug repellent at home. Fill a spray bottle with ½ cup of distilled water, ½-cup witch hazel, and 30 to 40 drops of your choice of citronella, clove, tea tree, mint, or eucalyptus essential oil.

Treat Toenail Fungus with Vicks VapoRub

Toenail fungus can be an embarrassing problem. The good news is that you can get rid of it with an easy and cheap treatment: Vicks VapoRub. The ingredients in Vicks VapoRub include camphor, menthol, eucalyptus oil, and thymol. These compounds have antifungal activity. Regularly applying Vicks VapoRub to nails infected with fungus has been shown to reduce and eventually eliminate toenail fungus.

Treat Sunburns with Tea

Gently apply chilled black tea or chamomile tea to the sunburn area to help soothe the skin. The tannins in black tea help soothe skin and speed the body's own recovery mechanism. Chamomile tea has anti-inflammatory properties that can help treat

Doodle to Improve Memory

Research suggests that doodling during a cognitive task helps improve memory because it keeps the brain stimulated. So go ahead and doodle, just be careful what you doodle on.

Drink Coffee to Combat Headache

Caffeine makes painkillers up to 40% more effective. Drink a cup of coffee with your painkiller to get rid of your headache faster.

Ease a Toothache

Apply clove oil on and around the aching tooth to relieve the pain.

Exercise On-the-Go

If you work in an office, try get up at least every hour and go for a walk. If you have an office with stairs, walk or run up and down the stairs every couple of hours. Get your blood flowing and your muscles moving.

Floss to Improve Brain Function

We all know the great benefits of flossing for oral health, but did you know it also helps brain health? Plaque that accumulates between your teeth can trigger an immune response that prevents arteries from getting nutrients to the brain.

Staying Healthy

Drink through a Straw to Stay Hydrated

If you struggle to drink your eight glasses of water a day, try slurping through a straw. Straws increase the volume of liquid that you drink because you can't see how much you are drinking.

Order Children's Portions

When ordering food at restaurants, order from the children's menu as an easy way to reduce calories and get your portion sizes under control.

Switch Plates

Research shows that having a large plate full of food will most likely lead to eating the entire thing. Cut calories by eating off a smaller plate. This optical illusion will trick your brain and will lead to the same feelings of satiety with fewer calories.

Spice Things Up

Spices like cayenne pepper, cinnamon, and ginger help you reach your weight loss goals. Studies show that spices like cayenne pepper, cinnamon, and cloves boost fat metabolism thanks to their ability to reduce insulin and triglyceride responses to food.

to your brain that make you want to eat more. Diet sodas can thus lead you to consume more calories and gain weight, instead of losing it.

Drink Grape Juice

Everyone knows that, in moderation, red wine has many health benefits. But too much alcohol can offset the benefits. If you find it hard to drink just one glass of wine or are trying to avoid alcohol altogether, try drinking dark grape juice. The resveratrol and flavonoids responsible for much of red wine's health benefits are also found in grape juice. So drink red grape juice as a healthy non-alcoholic alternative and have the health benefits without the alcohol.

Eat More Protein

Diets higher in protein and moderate in carbs have a higher potential for weight loss. Eating enough protein helps preserve muscle mass and encourages fat burning while keeping you feeling full.

Eat Negative Calorie Foods

Some foods actually burn more calories during digestion than they contain. Adding foods like celery, cauliflower, hot chili peppers, and zucchini can be a perfect addition to your weight loss efforts.

Weight Loss Tips

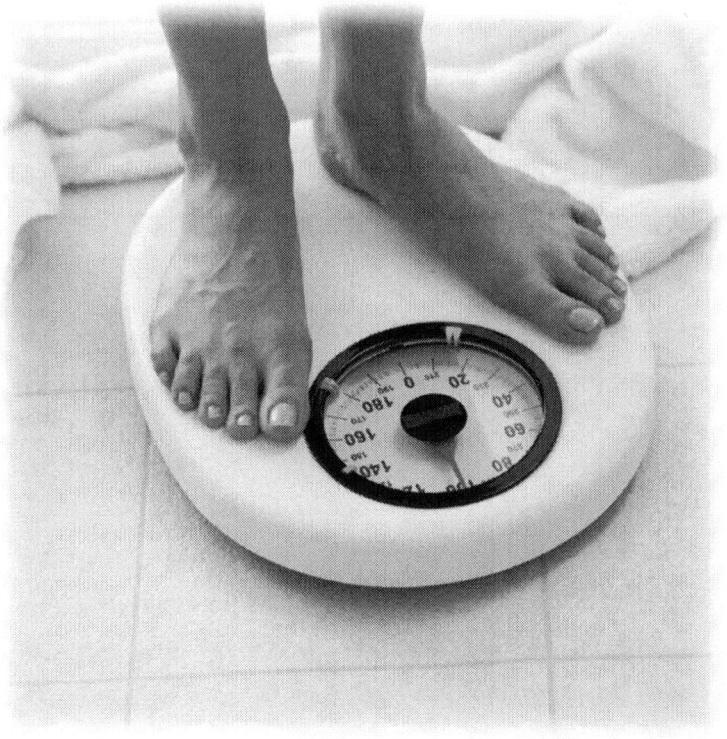

The keys to losing weight and getting fit are eating less and exercising more. Sounds simple enough, but we all know how difficult that can be in the context of real life and its demands. Here are some tips and tricks that can help you stay on track.

Ditch the Diet Soda

Diet sodas may have no calories, but they can kill your weight loss progress. Studies have shown that the artificial sweeteners in diet sodas send messages

6. Health and Wellness Tips

When it comes to being healthy and fit, it's the little things you do every day that make a difference. Here are a few tips and ideas to help you stay fit, healthy, and full of energy.

baking soda will serve to soften waters and alleviate skin irritation.

Sugar Spice Body Scrub

This luxuriously moisturizing sugar scrub smells good enough to eat. The sugar gently exfoliates and the almond oil and spices leave a subtle scent on the skin. Mix ¼ cup of brown sugar, ¼ cup of white sugar, 3 tablespoons of almond oil, and a pinch of ginger and nutmeg.

Vanilla Coconut Sugar Scrub

Coconut oil is subtly fragrant and super moisturizing. This wonderful scrub can practically double as dessert. Mix ¼ cup of coconut oil, ½ cup of brown sugar, and 1 teaspoon of vanilla. Rub on the skin while you shower and rinse.

tea (for hydration) while in the tub for an extra relaxing experience.

De-stress by Bathing in the Dark

End a particularly stressful day in a wonderful calming way with a candlelit bath or shower. Light your favorite sweet-smelling candles and turn all the lights off. By creating a quiet and calming ambiance associated with the candles and their smells, you can put yourself into a state of complete relaxation.

Refreshing Sea Salt Scrub

Mix in ¼ tablespoon of sea salt and 1 teaspoon of olive oil. Blend well. Next, squeeze ½ teaspoon of lemon juice into the mixture. Rub on the skin while you shower, massage and rinse. Not only is slathering this salt and oil scrub all over your body wickedly pleasant and invigorating, but the exfoliating factor also leaves your skin refreshed and vibrant.

Relaxing Bath Salts

After an exhausting day at work, there's nothing better than a nice hot bath enriched with fragrant bath salts. It's quite easy to prepare your own bath salt blend at home. In a large bowl, mix to ½ cup sea salt; ¼ cup Epson salts and 3 tablespoons of baking soda. Add a few drops of essential oils, and combine. The sea salts and Epson salt will soothe tired muscles and reduce inflammation and the

Body and Soul

You do not have to break the bank to enjoy a spa day and have beautiful pampered skin. Here are some refreshing homemade scrubs and body treatments that will bring your dull skin back to life.

Cleansing Detox Bath

You can detox heavy metals and other chemicals from the body with this gentle but effective cleansing detox bath. Start with a clean bathtub and fill it with hot water (as hot as you can comfortably tolerate). Add two cups of Epson Salt to draw out toxins and two cups of baking soda to neutralize the acids of the toxins in the water. Soak for half an hour. Read your favorite book and drink some hot

Whiten Nails

After removing dark nail polish, your nails may look stained. Whiten them by soaking them in a solution of hot water, baking soda and hydrogen peroxide.

bowl of ice-cold water for two minutes to freeze-dry your polish, sealing and hardening it quickly.

Protein Hair Treatment

For shiny hair and help with damaged or split ends, whisk together three eggs with one tablespoon of lemon juice. Apply to clean damp hair and leave it on for 15 minutes. Rinse with cool water.

Sexy Vacation Hair

If you love the way your hair looks and feels when you go to the beach, then you'll love this. Mix some sea salt and water in a spray bottle, add in a little leave-in conditioner, and spritz evenly over your hair. This will instantly give you sexy vacation hair!

Shine Enhancing Hair Mask

To restore shine to dull lifeless hair, mix one medium sized banana, mashed with a fork, 1 egg, beaten and 4 tablespoons of unflavored yogurt. Apply to hair and leave for 15 minutes.

Tame the Frizz in a Pinch

Are you out and about and your hair is looking frizzy? Rub some hand lotion through your hair to tame the frizz. Your hair and your hands will appreciate it!

Deep Conditioning Hair Mask

Add moisture and manageability to your hair by using this wonderful conditioning mask. Mix a mashed avocado and 2 tablespoons of coconut oil. Massage the mixture to your unwashed hair. Cover with a shower cap and let sit in hair for 20 minutes. Rinse thoroughly with cool water. The conditioning effects will be felt immediately.

Eliminate Static in Hair

Annoyed with static hair? Just rub a dryer sheet over the top of your head to smooth out the fly-aways.

Emergency Nail File

If you have a nail emergency and don't have access to nail file, use a matchbook striker as substitute nail file.

Long-Lasting Nail Polish

Make your nail polish last longer by soaking your fingernails for one minute in 1 cup of warm water and 1 to 2 tablespoons vinegar. When your nails dry, you can paint them as usual. This will remove oils often found on the nails and the nail polish will stick to the surface of the nails and not to the oils.

Quickly Dry Nail Polish

Paint your nails as usual and allow them to air-dry for two minutes. Then submerge your hands in a

Beautiful Hair and Nails

Your hair is regularly exposed to harmful elements such as pollution, sunshine, wind, and styling products, which cause split ends, coarse texture, and dull color. Deep conditioning treatments can do wonders to improve the texture of your hair. You don't have to spend a lot of money for salon treatments or store-bought products when you can revitalize the soft texture and shine of your hair at home.

Cleansing Rinse for Hair

To remove built up shampoo residues from your hair, mix enough baking soda and water to form a thick paste and use the mixture instead of shampoo about once week.

and sage in a saucepan and simmer for 10 minutes. Let it cool for a few minutes and strain out the sage. Mix the cooled liquid with the vodka in a jar. Dab the mixture with a cotton ball.

Yogurt Acne Treatment

Yogurt is full of vitamins and minerals that are not only healthy for the body but also for the complexion. The acidic nature of yogurt draws oil out from the surface of the skin and kills the bacteria that cause breakouts of the skin.

Mix a teaspoon of honey and a blob of yogurt. Blend it well. Apply the mixture to your face and wash it off after 10 minutes. You can also mix yogurt and sugar and use it as a scrub. You will love how your skin looks and feels!

Lip Exfoliator

Mix sugar and Vaseline to form a paste. Massage on lips to exfoliate and smooth dry, peeling lips.

Reduce Eye Puffiness

The skin around your eyes is very thin and very delicate. It must be treated with a gentle touch and great care. Cool temperatures naturally constrict blood vessels, which helps reduce puffiness and dark circles under the eyes. Almost everyone knows that slices of cucumber placed over the eyes for a few minutes will reduce puffiness. However, not everyone knows that using chilled used teabags will work just as well. As an extra benefit, the tannin in the tea also functions as a natural skin-tightener.

Smooth Shiny Legs

Add a little baby oil to your body lotion for super soft and smooth skin with just a touch of non-greasy glimmer.

Treat Blackheads and Oily Skin

Apply a mask of milk of magnesia once a week to keep oily skin and blackheads in check.

Vodka-Sage Astringent

This astringent can be used to help reduce oiliness and acne breakouts. Mix ½ cup of dried sage leaves, ½ cup of vodka, and 1 cup of water. Mix the water

Exfoliating Face Scrub

Exfoliating is a very important part of any skin care regime. This facial is mildly exfoliating, anti-bacterial, and moisturizing!

Mix ½ cup of brown sugar with ¼ cup of honey, stirring slowly. Mix in approximately 1 to 2 teaspoons of milk. Use the mixture to gently to exfoliate your skin, being careful to avoid the delicate skin around the eyes. Rinse the mixture off with warm water; be sure to clean extra well around your hairline or some of the honey might dry in sticky clumps.

Fix a Streaky Tan

Use lemon juice to smooth away unevenly applied sunless tanner. Lemon is a natural skin lightener and exfoliator. Sweep a cotton ball soaked in pure lemon juice over streaky areas.

Itchy Scalp Solution

If you suffer from uncomfortable dry, flaky scalp, use Listerine instead of expensive medicated shampoos. Dry flaky scalp is usually caused by built up oils and bacteria. The antiseptic ingredients in Listerine kill the built-up bacteria on the scalp. Dab or spray some Listerine directly on the scalp. Do not use on broken or open skin.

Banana Face Mask for Oily Skin

Bananas are another fantastic alternative for your oily skin. The vitamins and minerals will help to clear up blemishes and leave your skin feeling soft and smooth. Mash 1 ripe banana and mix in 1 teaspoon of honey and ½ teaspoon of fresh lemon juice. Apply to your face and let it rest for about 10 minutes. Remove with warm water and a washcloth.

Chamomile Toner

Use this wonderfully refreshing toner after cleansing. Mix half a cup of witch hazel with 1 cup of brewed chamomile tea. This tea can be used on dry, oily, or combination skin. It can be stored for up to 3 days in the refrigerator.

Conditioner Shaving Cream

There's no need to waste money buying separate shaving products to have smooth sexy legs. Just use your hair conditioner. It will serve to reduce nicks and cuts and leave your legs really smooth.

Cucumber Astringent

Peel and blend a medium cucumber. Strain the juice and remove the pulp. Mix the juice with a few drops of honey and stir. Use cotton balls to dab the mixture onto your face and enjoy the fresh tingly sensation. The cucumber will serve to tone your skin. You can refrigerate it and use for up to 4 days.

Beauty Tips and Ideas

Commercial beauty products out there are often filled with laboratory-concocted ingredients. Making these products at home is fun and easy. They are also a lot less expensive than commercial products or having a treatment at a spa. Here are a few easy ideas for you to try:

Amazing Oily Skin Scrub Cleanser

Dawn dish soap not only removes grease from dishes, but it is also a mild, yet effective grease remover for the skin. Mix a tablespoon of sugar with a few drops of Dawn dish soap and gently scrub the mixture on your face. This is a fantastic alternative to expensive oily-skin cleansers.

5. DIY Beauty and Pampering Ideas

Everyone needs a little "me" time. Women, especially, need that time to pamper themselves. It doesn't matter if it is late evening, night time, or early morning, take a little time to pamper and treat yourself well. Below are my favorite at-home spa tips and tricks for instant rejuvenation and a little self-pampering.

Home skin care is becoming more popular because of the rising prices for professional beauty products and services. Many women are discovering that their kitchens already contain many of the items that can keep their skin clean, healthy, and vibrant.

Use a Coat Rack

Hang your necklaces and bracelets within easy reach by draping them on the hooks of a wall-mounted coat rack.

Organize Your Linen Closet

Store bed-linen sets inside one of their own pillowcases and there will be no more hunting through piles to find a match.

Pillow Case Garment Bags

Convert your old pillowcases into garment bags. Cut an inch-wide slit at the center of the stitched end of the pillowcase. Slide the hanger hook through the slit and pull the pillowcase over the clothing article.

Repurposed Shoe Organizer

Hanging shoe organizers are not just for shoes! You can use these handy organizers for everything from keeping cleaning supplies to styling products and tools.

Use Bowls and Containers

The living room has many different uses, which might make it the hardest area to keep organized. The more loose items you have on surfaces, the more stuff will continue to collect there. To help keep your living room clutter-free, make use of bowls and containers as much as possible. Have decorative bowls, bins, and boxes that double as storage containers for loose items like keys, coins, and pens.

Color Code Your Keys

Tired of sorting through keys trying to figure out the correct one? Tell them apart by color-coding them with your favorite nail polish. Just lay them flat and apply a couple of coats to the top of each one. Use contrasting shades for each and have fun with it.

Fabric Drawer Pull

If you have a dresser with a missing drawer pull, try this wonderful fix: thread your favorite ribbon fabric through the holes and tie a knot on the inside to secure it in place.

Grocery Bag Dispenser

If you have grocery bags cluttering the area under your sink, use this clever idea to keep them organized and accessible. Stuff your empty grocery bags into an empty tissue box or plastic wet-wipes container to easily dispense your plastic grocery bags. Keep it under the sink and pull a bag out when you need it.

Ice Cube Tray as Drawer Organizer

Use old ice cube trays or empty egg cartons as drawer organizers for all of your hair accessories, jewelry, or other small odds and ends like buttons and safety pins.

4. Organizing Solutions and Ideas

No one is as organized as they wish they could be, so the promise of a more organized home life can be quite uplifting. The following ideas are practical and creative ways to use ordinary household items in unexpected ways to combat clutter and organize your home.

the rust stain and let it dry. You should then wash the item as usual.

Replace Hoodie or Sweatpants String

If you accidentally pulled your hoodie or sweatpants string out, stick the string in a straw and staple it. Use the straw to guide the string and easily loop the string back through.

Set Colors

Place new brightly colored cottons overnight in water with a ¼ cup of salt. Let it soak for several hours. This will help set the colors and keep them bright.

Wash the Washer

To keep your washing machine clean and smelling fresh, fill it with water and two cups of white vinegar. Let it sit for an hour and then run the machine and allow it to through the wash cycle.

Remove Stubborn Blood Stains

Use salt to remove bloodstains from clothes. Immerse the item in cold water and add lots of salt. Let the stained article soak for about 20 minutes and then rub with laundry soap.

Remove Lipstick Stain

Kiss that red smudge good-bye. Spray a little hairspray on the stain and let it sit for 15 minutes. Dab with a damp cloth to remove and then wash the garment with laundry detergent and a little baking soda.

Remove Permanent Marker from Clothes

If you accidently got some marker on your favorite shirt, it doesn't mean that your shirt is bound for the trash. Use hairspray or rubbing alcohol to remove marker stains from clothing. Moisten the stain with rubbing alcohol or non-oily hairspray and then blot away at it with a paper towel or clean white rag. You should begin to see the color from the marker transfer from the fabric to the paper towel. After the stain is removed, wash the clothing in the washing machine.

Remove Rust from Clothes

The citric acid in lemon oxidizes rust. To remove rust from clothes, apply some lemon juice and salt to

Get Rid Of Coffee Stains

Although this tip may sound strange, it really works: mix egg yolk and warm water and rub it into the coffee stain. Let it set for 2-3 minutes and watch the stain vanish.

Get Rid of Armpit Stains

To get rid of armpit stain on white shirts or tees, rub them with a mixture of 1 tablespoon dish soap, 3 teaspoons of hydrogen peroxide and 2 tablespoons of baking soda.

Make Your Own Dryer Sheet

Make your own dryer sheets that are both inexpensive and reusable. Cut an old cotton t-shirt or a couple reusable dishcloths into 4 by 4 squares. Mix ¼ cup of white vinegar with a couple drops of your favorite essential oil. The vinegar will work as a softener and the oil will give your clothes a pleasant, long lasting scent. Place the cloths in a sealable jar and pour the mixture over them until they are dampened but not soaked. Keep them in the sealed container.

Refresh and Re-fluff Your Pillows

Stick your flat or lumpy pillows in the dryer with a couple of tennis balls. In addition to the fluffing effect of the bouncing tennis balls, the heat will kill mold and germs.

Laundry Tips

Bright Whites

Do you have dingy whites that you wash time and time again...but never come out bright white anymore? Skip the bleach, and add ¼ cup of lemon juice to the wash cycle to brighten up those fading whites.

Dry Clothes Faster

Save energy and dry clothes faster. When you put a load in the dryer, throw in a clean, dry towel. The towel will absorb the moisture and the whole load will take much less time to dry.

Remove Wine Stains from Carpet

If you're freaking out because you just spilled a glass of red wine on your beige carpet, please don't panic. Club soda and vinegar will help you lift that stain right out, although you'll still have to do a little scrubbing. On a fresh stain, absorb the extra moisture by blotting it with a clean cloth. Dab it with vinegar to neutralize the red pigment. Then apply some club soda to the stain and let it sit for approximately 30 minutes. Gently blot the area with a wet cloth or sponge and then a dry cloth.

about four weeks if you used enough salt in the recipe to hold off the mold.

Refresh Your Old Potpourri

Has your potpourri lost its scent? You can refresh the scent by spritzing it with a little rubbing alcohol or vodka. Pour about ½ cup rubbing alcohol or vodka into a spray bottle. Spritz this over the top of potpourri and mix it up a bit. The alcohol will bring back the potpourri's original scent.

Removing Crayon Marks from Walls

Did your child create a work of art on your wall? You'll be able to remove these crayon marks by scrubbing them with toothpaste (not gel) and a cloth. Rinse and dry.

Remove Marker from Walls

Use hair spray or rubbing alcohol to remove magic marker or ink from your walls.

Remove Watermarks from Wood

Did your friend forget to use a coaster and now you a have an awful white ring on your wood table? Save the friendship, use mayonnaise to remove the watermark. Rub a tablespoon of mayonnaise on the water ring and let it sit for about 30 minutes. Wipe clean. It will look as if it never happened.

Homemade All Purpose Cleaner

With just a few simple ingredients, you can make your own nontoxic, all-purpose cleaner at home. Mix ½ gallon of hot water, ½-tablespoon baking soda, and 1-tablespoon dish soap in a spray bottle.

Make Your Own Air Freshener

You don't really need all those scented plug-ins, sprays, or automatic dispensers to keep your home feeling and smelling fresh.

Poke about 10-15 holes on the lid of an old canning jar with a hammer and nail. Place ½ cup of baking soda and a few drops of your favorite essential oil. The baking soda will absorb the unpleasant odors and the essential oil will provide a freshening, welcoming scent. Make several jars and place them in different areas of your home, such as your kitchen cabinets, closets, bathroom, etc.

You can also try to wonderfully clever alternative:

In a pot, add a few drops of your favorite essential oil and a few drops of food coloring to ½-cup water. Bring water to a boil and remove from heat. Dissolve 2 packets of plain gelatin and 2 tablespoons of salt into the hot water and then then add the other ½ cup of cold water. Stir well. Pour into jars and refrigerate. When the gelatin has completely set, cover with lids that have holes punched in them to allow the fragrance to escape. These should last litter absorbs the oil, you can clean up the litter with a broom and dustpan.

Dust Repellent

To keep dust off your furniture, mix one 2 tablespoons of liquid fabric softener with ½ cup water. Apply to furniture with a soft cloth and then dry with another cloth. This will repel dust.

Easy Wood Furniture Polish

Mix 6 tablespoons of olive oil with 3 tablespoons of lemon juice. Rub the mixture into the wood surface and let it sit for 15 minutes. Wipe with a soft dry cloth.

Get Rid of Musty Smells

Get rid of musty smells from old luggage or bins with kitty litter. Just pour half a box of kitty litter into the offending piece, close it, and leave it in there for several days.

Fabric Softener Sheets for Easy Dusting

Dusting your home is essential. It allows you to have a clean looking home, but it also helps remove pollen, pet dander, and other allergens. To save money and time, you can dust with used fabric softener sheets, which are electrostatic and attract dust as well as the expensive dusting cloths.

General Cleaning Tips

Clean a Narrow Vase with Alka-Seltzer

To clean a vase with a narrow neck, fill it halfway with water and drop in two Alka-Seltzer tablets. The baking soda and fizzing action in the Alka-Seltzer will do the dirty work for you.

Clean Up Grease Spills

If you spilled some grease or oil in your garage, pour kitty litter over the spill and grind the kitty litter with your foot to help break it up further. Once the

Leave on the toilet for about one hour and then flush. The citric acid contained in the lemon powder will oxidize the rust.

Remove Hard Water Buildup

To remove unsightly hard water buildup from your showerhead, fill a plastic bag with vinegar or fresh lemon juice and place it over showerhead. Hold the bag there with a rubber band. The acidity in vinegar or lemon juice will help dissolve the buildup.

Remove Soap Scum

Soap scum is a combination of residue, mineral deposits, and dirt that forms a grimy layer over surfaces. To remove it, pour ½ cup of boiling water, ½ cup of white vinegar, and a few squirts of liquid dish soap. Spray the area generously with this mixture and allow it to soak for about 10 minutes. Scrub clean and rinse well with water. Be careful when using on tile grout since vinegar may affect color.

paste. Use it with a brush or sponge to scour your bathtub and sink surfaces.

Defogging Bathroom Mirrors

Wipe some shaving cream on your mirrors and then wipe clean to keep them from fogging up in cold weather.

Easily Clean Shower Curtains

Soap scum can easily be removed from shower curtains. Put them in the washer with a couple of full size towels. Add ½ cup of vinegar and wash in gentle cycle.

Keep Drain Clog Free

To keep your drains clog-free and odorless, combine ¼-cup baking soda, ¼-cup table salt, and 2 tablespoons of cream of tartar. Stir ingredients together thoroughly and pour into drain, and immediately add 1-cup boiling water. Wait a few seconds and then flush with cold water. Do this weekly to keep your drains free of clogs.

Prevent Rust with Nail Polish

Coat the bottom of your shaving cream can to prevent rust rings on your bathtub ledge.

Remove Rust from Toilet Bowl

Every two to three weeks, sprinkle a packet of lemon Kool-Aid on the sides of the toilet and brush.

Bathroom Cleaning Tips

Cleaning the bathroom may be one of your least favorite chores, but it's something that has to be done. This section offers simple tips and techniques to make this task easier for you, so you can keep your bathroom sparkling clean.

Bathtub and Sink Cleaner

Mix one teaspoon of liquid laundry detergent with ½ cup of baking soda. Add enough water to form a

Remove Tarnish with Ketchup

Use ketchup to remove tarnish from copper and brass pots, pans, and fixtures. Dab ketchup onto a soft cloth and gently rub item. Rinse with warm water.

Stainless Steel Polisher

There's no need to buy expensive stainless steel cleaners. Use car wax to keep stainless steel appliances smudge and fingerprint free. Apply a thin coat of car wax to fridge, stove, or other appliances and buff clean.

Unclog Your Drain or Garbage Disposal

If your drain or garbage disposal is clogged, instead of using harsh chemical drain cleaner, pour some Coke down the drain and wait for it to stop fizzing, and then rinse with hot water. The phosphoric acid in cola breaks down the gunk removing the blockage safely and effectively.

Sparkling Pans

Clean your pans, stove, and stainless steel appliances with baking soda and hydrogen peroxide. Pour ¼ cup of baking soda in a bowl, add enough peroxide to make a thick paste and rub on with a sponge.

Microwave Cleaning Shortcut

The quickest way to clean a microwave oven is to place a couple of wet paper towels inside and nuke them for about 3 minutes. The steam from the towels will soften the grime. Once the paper towels cool down, use them to wipe the oven's interior.

Remove Burnt Smell from Kitchen

If you burned a dish and want to get rid of that awful smell, boil some lemon slices in pan for 5 minutes.

Restore Your Tarnished Silverware

To polish tarnished silverware, boil 8 cups of water and ¼ cup of baking soda. Line a large pan with aluminum foil. Add your silverware to the lined pan and pour the boiling solution over them, making sure to cover the silverware completely. Once the water has cooled, remove the items and rinse with cool water. You can now wipe them with a clean cloth and marvel at their beautiful restored shine.

Clean Cast Iron with Salt

Most cooks know that you should never use soap to clean a cast-iron pan. So how do you clean it? Use salt. Add a couple tablespoons of vegetable oil and 3 tablespoons of salt. Using a paper towel, scour until clean. Then rinse and coat with oil to cure.

Clean Stove Burners without Scrubbing

If you have unsightly grease and spatter cooked onto your burners, you can clean it without scrubbing. Put each burner into a Ziploc bag and add a ¼ cup of ammonia to each bag. You don't need a lot of ammonia; the fumes will do the hard work. Leave the burners sealed in the bags overnight. The ammonia fumes will dissolve the grease and hardened oil. Take them out of the bags and wipe them clean with a sponge. You will be amazed!

Warning: Do not mix the ammonia with other cleaners, especially bleach. Mixing ammonia with bleach will create toxic fumes.

Eliminate Fridge Odors

If you wrinkle your nose every time you open your fridge, even after you've cleaned it, try lining your drawers with newspaper. Newspaper will absorb the odors and will keep your produce dry so it will last longer.

Kitchen Cleaning Tips

Keeping your kitchen clean isn't exactly fun, but it doesn't have to be drudgery either. Here is a great collection of clever tips and hints that will help make cleaning your kitchen easier and more efficient. Tackle the tough spots on your kitchen countertops, appliances, and pots using common items you already have on hand.

Clean Blender Pitcher Easily

After using the blender, rinse the pitcher and fill it about ¼ full with warm water. Add a squirt of dish soap and put it back on the blender. Run the blender for 30 seconds. Rinse it out again and you're done!

3. Cleaning Tips and Tricks

A clean and well-kept home is a place where you can truly relax and feel happy. Your home can be a place that makes you forget the stress and hard work of the day. However, keeping your home clean and tidy usually requires good deal of time, money, and effort.

Here are a few clever tips and tricks that will help you save money and reduce both the time and effort required to keep your house clean. They are easy and simple and will make your home more pleasant and your life much easier

Overly Sweet Foods

Cut the sweetness in over sugared foods by adding a squeeze of lemon or a few drops of vinegar.

Over Greasy Stew or Sauce

When making a soup, sauce, or casserole that ends up too greasy or fatty, drop in an ice cube. The ice cube will attract the fat, which you can then scoop out.

Popcorn That Won't Pop

If your popcorn kernels won't pop, it's likely because they dried out. You need to add moisture back. Soak the kernels in water for a few minutes, drain and pat them dry with a paper towel.

warm oven for about five minutes. The meat should regain some of its moisture.

Curb the Acidic Bite

Is your sauce or dressing too acidic? Add a small pinch of baking soda to neutralize the sting without adding unwanted flavor.

Fix Mushy Pasta

If you've overcooked your pasta, don't worry, it's not the end of the world. You can get that "al dente" feel back by quickly sautéing it in a pan with a little olive oil.

Over-Baked Cookies

Are your cookies not as soft as you intended? Put them in a plastic container with a slice of bread and leave them for about 24 hours. The cookies will absorb the moisture from the bread and become soft and gooey. Putting them in the microwave for about 5 seconds can also do the trick.

Over-Salted Food

You can add a little bit of sugar or vinegar to balance out the brine of a dish that has been over-salted. If you are making a soup, drop in a peeled cut potato and it will absorb the excess salt.

Correct Cooking Mistakes

Even the most experienced cooks can make mistakes in the kitchen, so don't beat yourself up or throw that dish out. Whether you over-salted or overcooked your dish, you can use some simple techniques and ingredients to hide your mistake and balance out the flavors.

Add Moisture Back to Overcooked Meat

Did you overcook your meat and it's now a little dry? To remedy this, pour the drippings into a pan, add 1 or 2 cups of stock, and bring it to a boil. Cut the meat in smaller portions and place it in a roasting pan or baking dish. Add the stock mixture and cover it with a lid or foil. Place it in a

Use Cookie Cutters for Pancakes

Give your kids (or spouse) a special Sunday morning treat by making fun shaped pancakes. Whip up a batch of your favorite pancake recipe and heat up the griddle or frying pan. Place the metal cookie cutters on the hot griddle and spray the insides with cooking spray. Pour the batter into the cookie cutters. Remove the cookie cutters with tongs before flipping the pancake.

Vegetable Ice Cubes

Instead of throwing out your leftover vegetables, puree them in a blender and pour them into ice cube trays. Use them to flavor stews or soups.

two more paper towels. Place in the microwave and cook for 3 to 4 minutes. Check for crispiness at one-minute intervals. When ready, toss the towels for easy cleanup.

Revive Crystallized Honey

To bring honey back to its smooth and drizzly state, place the container in a bowl of hot water for about 5 minutes.

Roast Chicken with Legs Facing Back

The legs of the chicken take the longest time to cook. Because the back corners of the oven become the hottest, it will ensure that they are cooked evenly with the rest of the chicken.

Restore Milk Freshness

If your milk has just started to turn sour, pour in a pinch of baking soda to restore freshness.

Soften Brown Sugar

As moisture evaporates, brown sugar can become hard over time. You can easily add moisture back by placing the open sugar bag in a microwave with a cup of water next to it and zapping it for 2 minutes.

vegetables to rot. It will also make cleaning the bins much easier.

Make Dumpling Wrappers with White Bread

Instead of buying dumpling dough or having to make them from scratch, you can easily make dumpling wrappers with soft white bread instead. Start by cutting off the crusts, flatten the bread with a rolling pin, then stuff, fold, pinch, and cook them same way you would regular dumpling wrappers.

Mold-Free Berries

Berries are quite delicate and can become moldy very quickly. It can be quite disappointing to bring home fresh tasty berries only to find them covered in mold just a few days later. If you want your berries to last a week or more, rinse them with vinegar to keep them from becoming moldy and mushy. Prepare a mixture of one part vinegar and ten parts water. Place the berries in the mixture and swirl them around. Drain, rinse, and store them in the fridge. The vinegar destroys the mold spores and bacteria that might be on the surface of the fruit.

No-Mess Bacon

Layer two paper towels on a flat plate. Lay slices of bacon side by side on the paper towels. Cover with minutes and then peel. The baked eggs will easier to peel and have a creamier texture. Enjoy!

Ice Cold Beer in 10 Minutes

You can make your canned or bottled drinks ice cold in just a few short minutes. Place your bottles or cans in a container (preferably an ice chest). Cover them with plenty of ice, add sufficient water to cover them completely, and top off the ice with plenty of salt (half a cup for 6 beers). In 10 to 15 minutes you will have ice cold drinks.

When salt is added to water, it lowers the temperature at which that water will freeze. The more salt the water contains, the lower its freezing point will be. When you add salt, the water is cooling to temperatures below zero while still staying liquid. That is why it chills the bottles much faster than regular ice and water.

Keep Dairies Fresh

Store sealed yogurt, sour cream, and cottage cheese upside down; this will make them last up to one week longer!

Keep Produce Fresh

Line your vegetable drawer with paper towels so your vegetables will stay fresher longer. The paper towels absorb the moisture that causes your ice cream as smooth and soft as when you first bought it.

Fresh Herbs All Year Round

Preserve the fresh taste of your herbs by freezing them in oil. Rinse your herbs thoroughly, cut off the long stems on herbs like cilantro or parsley. Finely chop your fresh herbs and mix ¼ cup of olive oil to 1 cup of chopped herbs. Put mixture in a zip-lock freezer bag. Flatten and distribute the mixture evenly to achieve a thin layer. Freeze flat. Once frozen, you'll be able to break off pieces as needed. For the freshest taste, be sure to use within 6 months.

Get More Juice from Lemons

Before cutting the lemon, place it in pan with water and bring to a boil. You will be surprised; you'll be able to get almost double the juice from it when you warm it up.

Hard Boiled Eggs in the Oven

Cooking a dozen or more perfect hard-boiled at once couldn't be easier with this hands-off method. Preheat your oven to 325-350° F (depending on your oven). Place the eggs in a muffin pan to prevent them from rolling around and bake them for 30 minutes. Remove the eggs and place them in cold water to stop the cooking process. Let them sit in the cold water for a few

Better Tasting Corn

For delicious tasting corn on the cob, add a tablespoon of sugar to the boiling water. The sugar will help bring out the corn's natural sweetness.

Chill Iced Tea with Fruit

Instead of ice cubes to chill your iced tea or lemonade, which can dilute your drink, try frozen fruit instead. The frozen fruit will keep the drink cold without adding excess water and will add a nice subtle flavor to your drink.

Crisp Wilted Lettuce

If your lettuce is a little wilted, don't throw it out. You can crisp wilted lettuce by submerging it in a bowl of ice-cold water and adding a couple of spoonful of cider vinegar. Let it stand for 10 to 15 minutes.

Easily Peel Boiled Eggs

When making hard-boiled eggs, add a little bit of vinegar to the water. The vinegar will soften the eggshells and make peeling the eggs much easier.

Frost-Free Ice Cream

To prevent unappealing frosty crystals from forming on your favorite ice cream, store the container in a large Ziploc bag. This will keep the

Food Preparation Tips and Ideas

Bake Potatoes Faster

Whether topped with a scoop sour cream or a simple pat of butter, baked potatoes are a favorite no-fuss meal. However, many find that baking potatoes just takes too long. There's an easy way to cut the baking time in half. Wash the potatoes and poke a few holes in them with a fork. Put the potatoes in hot water and let them stand for 10 minutes. They will require about half the time to bake.

2. Cooking Solutions

Whether you are just starting out in the kitchen and need help rescuing a ruined dish, or you are an experienced chef looking for tips and ideas to improve your cooking, this has some smart advice and ideas that we hope make cooking a more fun and fulfilling experience for you! You'll be a better, smarter cook with these clever tips. Bon Appetit!

members at a discount. Co-ops often carry mostly local and organic produce.

Grow Your Own

If you're serious about fresh organic produce, why not grow your own organic vegetables and herbs?

the day, as farmers will likely cut their prices, so they do not have to take their produce back to the farm.

Buy Store Brand Products

Stores like Publix, Wholefoods, and Trader Joe's carry their own brand of organic products. Regardless of the brand, they are all required to follow the same USDA organic certification guidelines.

Use Your Freezer

Frozen organic fruits and vegetables at the store are often cheaper than fresh, especially if the produce is out of season. You can also save by buying organic produce when in season in bulk and freeze it for later seasons.

Buy In Bulk

Whether you're shopping at a natural foods store or supermarket, buying in bulk is a great way to stretch your food dollar. Buy in-season produce and unpackaged foods such as nuts, oats, dried fruit, and legumes in bulk.

Join a Co-Op.

Co-ops are member-owned businesses that provide groceries and other products to its

Buying Organic on a Budget

Much of the food found in grocery stores is highly processed or even genetically modified. They are often grown using pesticides, hormones, and antibiotics. Many of us instinctively know that buying quality organic food and eating the most nutritious foods is the best thing for us. But let's face it, organic food can be quite expensive. If you see the benefits of switching to organic foods but are turned off by the price, these great tips will let you enjoy the freshness and goodness of organic foods without breaking your budget.

Shop at Farmer's Markets

Find a farmers market near you and get to know your local farmers; create a personal relationship and negotiate prices. Try to go toward the end of

Watch for Pricing Errors

Watch prices at the register and check your receipt before you leave the store to make sure no items were rung up incorrectly. Grocery stores update their prices on thousands of items every week, creating plenty of opportunities for pricing errors during checkout. Some stores such as Publix will give you the item free if you are overcharged, but it's up to you to catch the error.

policy. Many stores allow you to double up on coupons (store coupon + manufacturer coupon) and often even accept competitors' coupons.

Know Your Supermarkets Sale Cycle

Many products are put on sale on a regular cycle (generally 6 to 8 weeks). If an item is on sale this week, it will likely go on sale again in another 6 to 8 weeks. Pay attention to your stores sale cycle and buy enough of the sale item now to get you to the next sale and you won't ever have to pay full price for it again.

Walk to the Left

When you enter your supermarket, walk to the left instead of the right. Stores often will have their pricier products on the right side of the store because most shoppers walk that way first.

Shop on Wednesday

Wednesdays are a great time to get your hands on markdown items. Department managers usually markdown foods nearing their "sell by" date midweek. In addition, supermarkets usually put out their new circulars on Wednesdays, so you get a double bonus because they will usually honor last week's offers, too.

1. Grocery Shopping Tips and Hints

Save Big at the Supermarket

As a shopper, you must diligently look for ways to save money at the supermarket. Here are some great ideas that will help get more food and spend less money.

Clip Coupons

Clip all the grocery coupons you can find. Grab store discount fliers at every opportunity. Check the Sunday newspaper and even the inside of food packages. Pay attention to your stores coupon

Introduction

Are you exhausted by the great deal of effort and money required to take care of your home, car, and everything else in your busy life? Are you looking for ideas and solutions to make your home and life run a little smoother? This book is full of clever ideas, solutions, and inspiration to help you do just that.

Whether you are looking for ways to save money on your next trip, thinking of tackling a tough stain, embarking on some deep cleaning, or looking for simple ways to pamper yourself, this book will show you how.

Here you will find more than a hundred simple and effective solutions that will save you time and money so you can do more of the things you love. These clever tips and tricks have been tried and tested by moms, grandmothers, housekeepers, savvy travelers and other clever people who also wanted to solve problems, save money and just make their lives easier.

Some of the tips and ideas covered in the book have been around for a long time and may be familiar to you, but many others will be little known gems that will surprise you. I hope that you enjoy these clever ideas and that they save you time, money and effort, making *your life a little easier.*

7. Travel Hints and Tips 60

Money Saving Tips and Ideas 62

Packing Tips and Ideas 66

Breeze Through the Airport 70

Enjoy Your Trip More 74

8. Online Shopping Tips 77
9. Productivity Solutions 80
10. Car Tips and Solutions 83
Conclusion 88

Table of Contents

Introduction i

1. Grocery Shopping Tips and Hints 1

Save Big at the Supermarket 1

Buying Organic on a Budget 4

2. Cooking Solutions 7

Food Preparation Tips and Ideas 8

Correct Cooking Mistakes 15

3. Cleaning Tips and Tricks 18

Kitchen Cleaning Tips 19

Bathroom Cleaning Tips 23

General Cleaning Tips 26

Laundry Tips 31

4. Organizing Solutions and Ideas 35

5. DIY Beauty and Pampering Ideas 39

Beauty Tips and Ideas 40

Beautiful Hair and Nails 45

Body and Soul 49

6. Health and Wellness Tips 52

Weight Loss Tips 53

Staying Healthy 56

Copyright © 2013 by Naya Lizardo

All rights reserved. This book or any portion thereof may not be reproduced or used in any manner whatsoever without the express written permission of the author except for the use of brief quotations in a book review.

Printed in the United States of America

First Printing, 2013

ISBN-13. 978-1484129548

ISBN-10. 1484129547

REAL CLEVER
SOLUTIONS & IDEAS

Tips and Tricks to Save You Time and Money

Naya Lizardo